D0893345

AUTUMN YEARS

AUTUMN YEARS

Taking the Contemplative Path

ROBERT H. KING &
ELIZABETH M. KING

continuum

NEW YORK • LONDON

2004

The Continuum International Publishing Group Inc
15 East 26 Street, New York, NY 10017

The Continuum International Publishing Group Ltd
The Tower Building, 11 York Road, London SE1 7NX

www.continuumbooks.com

All biblical quotations are from the New Revised Standard Version unless otherwise noted.

"The Bright Field" from *Collected Poems* by R. S. Thomas (London: J. M. Dent, 2001), p. 87, is reprinted by permission of The Orion Publishing Group.

Printed in the United States of America

Library of Congress Cataloging-in-Publication Data

King, Robert Harlen, 1935-
    Autumn years : taking the contemplative path / by Robert H. King and Elizabeth M. King.
        p. cm.
    Includes bibliographical references.
    ISBN 0-8264-1639-X (alk. paper)
    1. Aged – Religious life. 2. Contemplation. I. King, Elizabeth M., 1930- II. Title.
BL625.4.K56 2004
204'.35'0846 – dc22

2004005684

Dedicated to the memory of
H. Q. and Mary Louise Banta
Grace, Helen, Howard, Lola, and Lila

Contents

Acknowledgments

We are especially grateful to our contemplative teachers, who have contributed so much to our own spiritual growth, and whose teachings are, either directly or indirectly, represented in this book.

Ben Wren introduced Robert to Zen meditation, and Shodo Harada Roshi of Sogenji Temple in Japan has been a continuing teacher for him. The late Fr. Joseph B. Smerke, OSC, introduced Elizabeth to Christian contemplative practice, and Yozan Dirk Mosig of Kearney, Nebraska, taught her Zen meditation. We are both very much indebted to our present Zen teachers, Joan Sutherland and David Weinstein.

We'd especially like to thank Joan for her "Harvest Questions," which appear in chapter 9, as well as for her support and guidance along the way.

We are grateful to Frank Oveis, senior editor of Continuum International, for his encouragement and his valuable suggestions for the shaping of this work. We also wish to thank Roger Cox for his careful reading of the manuscript and thoughtful comments.

To the Reader

Autumn Years is written in the form of a conversation between a husband and wife and you, the reader. So that you will know who the speaker is at any one time, we have adopted the following pair of symbols:

Oak Leaf   Maple Leaf

Robert   Elizabeth

To maintain gender neutrality when speaking generically, Robert will use the masculine pronoun and Elizabeth the feminine form.

The Bright Field

I have seen the sun break through
to illuminate a small field
for a while, and gone my way
and forgotten it. But that was the pearl
of great price, the one field that had
the treasure in it. I realize now
that I must give all that I have
to possess it. Life is not hurrying
on to a receding future, nor hankering after
an imagined past. It is the turning
aside like Moses to the miracle
of the lit bush, to a brightness
that seemed as transitory as your youth
once, but is the eternity that awaits you.

R. S. THOMAS

CHAPTER ONE

Flaming Colors, Falling Leaves

Lord it is time. The summer was immense.
Stretch out your shadow on the sundial's face,
And on the meadows let the wind go free.

RAINER MARIA RILKE

On my first trip to Japan in the fall of 1994, I was introduced to Yoshiei Shimizu. He was a very cultured man about my age, the head of a foundation but also a lecturer in Japanese civilization at one of the major universities in Tokyo. Responding to my interest in Japanese religion, he offered to take me to see an ancient Buddhist temple near the town of Shimada on the southern coast of Japan. The reason for visiting this particular temple was that it had on display an image of Kannon, the "bodhisattva of great compassion." *Bodhisattva* is the Buddhist term for a fully enlightened being who foregoes Nirvana in order to save other beings. This particular image is known as the "thousand-armed Kannon" because it has arms reaching in all directions to signify boundless compassion. What made the visit especially significant was that this image is only taken out and put on display once every sixty years. The rest of the time it is concealed behind a partition. Even the monks who belong to the temple are not permitted to see it except at this time, and then only for a few weeks.

The image was quite small and obviously very old, dating back to the founding of the temple in the eighth century. It could have been even older, since it did not appear at all Japanese, or even Chinese. More than likely it came from India, where Buddhism originated. I did not count the arms, but there were certainly a lot of them. Observing the image in its traditional setting — an ancient wood and stone temple set within a bamboo forest several hundred feet up the side of a mountain on a day when the rain was gently falling all around — was an awesome experience. I was deeply moved, and even with my Christian upbringing instinctively placed my hands together in *gassho* and reverently bowed to this sacred image.

On our way back to Tokyo, I asked Mr. Shimizu what was the significance of bringing the image out only every sixty years. Why wait so long between viewings? He explained that the Japanese, following the Chinese calendar, consider sixty years a complete lifetime. As anyone who has eaten at a Chinese restaurant in the United States is likely to know, this calendar is based on a twelve-year cycle with each year named for a different animal. (For instance, I was born in the year of the dog.) What I had not known before was that five cycles is considered a normal lifetime. Thus, the Japanese make a great point of celebrating a person's sixty-first birthday, since it marks the first year of that person's "new life." My friend observed that he was sixty years old and beginning to think about what he might do in the next period of his life. I told him I would soon turn sixty. The thought that this marker event might constitute a new beginning was an intriguing idea.

I had always assumed that I would retire at sixty-five, the age at which my father retired and until the mid-1980's the mandatory retirement age for most professions. When Congress eliminated the mandatory retirement age as a form of age discrimination, it made a temporary exception for tenured professors, but even that exception had expired. Nowhere did it say any longer that I had to retire at a particular age. This "freedom of choice" put me in something of a quandary. What was I to do with the rest of my life? Until then my profession had, for the most part, defined my life. Once I decided upon an academic career, I knew pretty much what I had to do to succeed. Yet there were no rules for success in retirement. There weren't even any guidelines or role models. I would have to make my own way. It was then that I began to think seriously about what I might look forward to in my Autumn Years.

How Old Is Old?

 A new life at age sixty. Something to look forward to? There was a time when I wouldn't have believed it. When I was thirty-five years old, I wrote an article about my sudden realization, one day, that "my life was half over." And I think I believed it to be true. I thought of my little, white haired, bent-over Grandmother Banta, with her veiny hands and thread-thin voice, who died at age seventy-one. Somehow, I didn't ever expect to get that old. Now here I am, a year past Grandmother's age, and I still feel about forty (most of the time!). I guess I just haven't bothered to update my internal calendar since mid-life. It may be about time, don't you think? When I hear TV commentators talking about Medicare and using the phrase, "this nation's elderly," I have to blink my eyes to realize they're talking about me! Well, maybe that's all right. So much depends on thoughts — habitual ways of thinking. I've long held as true the beginning of the ancient Buddhist text *The Dammapada:* "We are what we think, having become what we thought." I just may go on thinking of myself as about forty! What could it hurt?

And maybe I really *am* about the equivalent age of my own grandmother when she was forty! According to the MacArthur Foundation study on aging, "life expectancy at birth in the

United States has increased from forty-seven years in 1900 to approximately seventy-six years today."[1] Furthermore, the average American who has reached age sixty-five can expect to live seventeen more years. And for some unexplained reason, women are still living about seven years longer than men.

An even more significant finding of the MacArthur study is that people are not only living longer but are in better health, so these extra years can be fulfilling instead of debilitating. Here are the statistics. "Of those aged sixty-five to seventy-four in 1994, a full 89 percent report no disability whatsoever" and of those "between the ages of seventy-five to eighty-four, 73 percent still report no disability, and even after age eighty-five, 40 percent of the population is fully functional."[2] There are many more who have only minor disabilities and can therefore look forward to a very satisfying life during their Autumn Years.

Of course, many of us are beginning to notice some short-term memory loss. I have sometimes read a whole chapter of a book and failed to recall what I read a week later! I've been known to arrive at the grocery store with my list still posted on the refrigerator, or forget to return a phone call, or wonder what it was I went downstairs to get. But there is some encouraging news in this department as well! "Research has demonstrated the remarkable and enduring capacity of the aged brain to make new connections, absorb new data, and thus acquire new skills."[3] Studies have shown that we can even be trained to increase our short term memory by using mnemonic devices such as association and mental listing, as well as memory practice games. Crossword puzzles and games such as Scrabble can help us to retain and even increase our vocabulary. Memorization creates new connections in the brain, increasing the capacity of the network that's available for holding on to new material. I enjoy poetry so I sometimes memorize favorites. Not only is it nice to have a few poems available to savor or share, but I just may be helping my memory in the process. I have found, though, that it's necessary to keep coming back to these newly-memorized pieces in order to maintain what I've learned. Otherwise, they do begin to slip away. Yet it's awfully nice to know that there is something I can do to keep my mind in reasonable condition during this "new life" of my Autumn Years.

In addition to increased longevity and better memory retention, the Autumn Years can also gift us with the joy of coming to know our grown children as adults and friends. Although Robert's and my adult children are geographically scattered, we keep up a steady e-mail correspondence and stay in close touch by frequent phone calls and visits. And there's an added bonus: the great delight of grandchildren. Between the two of us, we have eleven grandchildren to love and enjoy. They help us to retain our youthful outlook and give us hope for the future as well as increased reason for living.

Successful Aging

Yet in our youth-oriented society, it is still quite common to think that there is nothing more to look forward to in one's later years than physical and mental decline, a steady downward projection of expectation. The Mac-Arthur study counters this view with a strategy for what it calls "successful aging." There are three components to this strategy:

1. avoiding disease and disability,

2. maintaining mental and physical function,

3. continuing engagement with life.

These three components are interrelated in that the "absence of disease and disability makes it easier to maintain mental and physical function, [while] maintenance of mental and physical function in turn enables (but does not guarantee) active engagement with life."[4]

Vulnerability to disease and disability is obviously not something that is entirely within our control, yet we now know that there is a great deal we can do in the way of diet, exercise and periodic medical screening to avoid the primary risks to healthy living in the later years: cancer, heart disease, stroke and osteoporosis. Likewise there is a certain inevitable diminishment of physical and mental power that goes with aging; yet, as Elizabeth observed, there are also things we can do to keep ourselves mentally and physically fit. For instance, I used to play golf regularly, but now I walk a mile or two a day and work in the garden. One of the surprising results of recent studies on aging is the finding that moderate physical activity can be as beneficial as strenuous exercise in maintaining vital mental and physical functions. Successful aging, it seems, does not require superhuman effort, just good sense and persistence.

The third component of successful aging, *continued engagement with life,* is in some respects the most interesting. Thirty years ago, according to the authors of this study, the prevailing view among gerontologists was something called "disengagement theory."

> This theory defined the main task of old age as letting go. The argument was that old age was a time at which people were required to give up their jobs, could no longer take part in the more strenuous forms of recreation, and sadly, had to say farewell to many old friends and family members. The final act of relinquishment was letting go of life itself.[5]

This theory is much less influential today, when it is coming to be recognized that older people should continue to maintain close personal relationships and remain involved in activities that are meaningful and purposeful. These relationships and activities, the study finds, are no less important to personal wellbeing in later life than in earlier years.

While I do not entirely disagree with this statement, I believe something important is missing. Nothing is said about cultivating the *inner* life. For some people in the Autumn Years it may be enough to keep up friendships and pursue meaningful work in order to remain engaged. Others, however, may feel a yearning for something more — a deeper engagement with life, a fuller self-understanding, a richer spiritual life. For such folks the Autumn Years could offer a unique opportunity for personal growth of a sort not available at any other time in life. As a society, we recognize that certain tasks are more appropriate at certain times in life, tasks such as pursuing an education, building a career, raising children, and assuming leadership responsibilities, but we do not, as a society, assign any particular task to the later years. We assume that people at this stage of life will simply disengage or, as this study recommends, continue doing what they were doing with some minor modifications. Yet there are other possibilities.

Becoming a Forest Dweller

For many years I taught in a college department of philosophy and religion. When I started, my interests were focused almost entirely on Christian theology. But the needs of my department required that I also teach a course in comparative religions. In that way I became acquainted with the major Eastern religions, in particular Hinduism and Buddhism. One of the ideas I encountered in my study of Hinduism especially interested me. It had to do with the *stages of life*. In traditional Hindu thought, a person's life can be divided into four distinct periods or stages. What interested me about this scheme was that it provided for something not present in our society, a period of spiritual growth following the completion of one's social responsibilities.

According to the Hindus, the first stage of life for a young man born into the upper caste of society is the "student stage." (Traditionally no provision was made for educating women or men of the lower castes.) Once a young man has attained the age of reason, he is assigned to a teacher, who instructs him in the sacred texts until such time as he is ready to assume the duties of a "householder." This is the second stage of life, when he is expected to marry and raise a family, ordinarily taking up the profession of his father. He remains in the householder stage until his own son is able to replace him. When he has "gray hairs and grandchildren," according to one of the ancient texts, he is formally discharged from these responsibilities. He is free to go off and become what Hindus call a "forest dweller." He might not literally live in a forest, but he is free to pursue his own spiritual development unencumbered by social obligations.

The forest dweller is expected to live an ascetic life, which means devoting himself single-mindedly to study and meditation with the object of achieving an advanced state of spiritual development free from worldly attachments. That's a pretty tall order, but there is another stage beyond even that of the forest dweller (though some scholars think it might originally have been another version of the same stage) called the *sannyasin*. The sannyasin is someone who has advanced so far spiritually that he no longer has any attachments. He is free to return to the community or live apart. Either way he is regarded with reverence as the epitome of the fully developed person.

These are idealized stages, which we may assume few men in Indian society ever fully attain. But at least the scheme envisions the possibility of human beings (women as well as men) developing spiritually in their later years, and that is a radical idea given the assumptions of our society. Perhaps the Hindus have something to teach us about aging. Could it be that inner, spiritual development is the special task of this time in life, that the Autumn Years are especially suited to personal spiritual growth, that there is a place for this forest dweller in our modern society? That is a possibility Elizabeth and I would like to explore.

A Circle of Seasons

Robert has written about the Japanese belief that life begins anew at age sixty and the Hindu custom of valuing the forest dweller stage of life as a time for spiritual growth. Christianity also has a tradition that honors the Autumn Years as a season for realizing the sacredness of life. It stems from the Celtic branch of Christianity, a tradition I first became interested in through reading the writings of John O'Donohue.

The Celtic Christians are a devout people with a sense of the divine Presence in all things. They see life as a *circle of seasons*, envisioning the stages of life as a circle in the same way that the four seasons are circular, each flowing into the next in an endlessly unbroken chain. Perhaps you have seen the Celtic cross, with its circle at the center accenting the intersection point of the vertical and the horizontal bars. One interpretation of this circle is as a symbol of eternity, which encompasses the whole of life and is without beginning or end.

Though the circle of seasons can be entered at any point, let's begin with winter. Just as a baby spends its first months in the womb preparing for birth, nature also requires a time of seclusion before new life can begin. During the winter, nature goes underground in order to gain strength for the new life that is to come in the spring. Each time a child is born, the world begins anew. All is fresh, all is growing. This is spring. The summer of life is for blooming and cultivating one's life. But autumn is the best season of all. It is the time of the soul's great harvest, a time when "aging invites us to become aware of the sacred circle that shelters our life."[6] It is the time of the inner harvest, when one can revisit memory's storehouse for the purpose of healing old pain and enjoying the fruits of the seeds planted in the spring and summer of life.

A sacred circle. I like the feeling of wholeness it carries. For me, it coincides with an inner shift in the way I think of the soul. Instead of seeing it as something ephemeral and inside the body, I've come to sense that, in fact, *the body is within the vast, all-pervading Soul!* Sometimes I'm able to live in awareness of that solid, beginningless and endless essence that surrounds me like the circle on the Celtic cross. These moments are fleeting, but I know that the gift of their truth is more solid and lasting than these thinning bones. There is a part of each of us that lives mainly in eternity. Even as our body ages, our soul can become a refuge, deepening and enriching our lives. Just like the Celtic knot that is without beginning or ending, time and eternity are woven together in our lives. John O'Donohue expresses this beautifully in his book *Anam Cara:*

> Age, as the harvest of life, is a time when your [planting and your tending] come to fruition. In this way, you unify yourself and achieve a new strength, poise, and belonging that was never available to you when you were distractedly rushing through your days. [The Autumn of life is] a time of coming home to your deeper nature, of entering fully into the temple of your memory where all your vanished days are secretly gathered and awaiting you.[7]

I find that these Autumn Years have invited me to partake of a new way of living — a quiet, gentle way, a deep, transcendent way — a way called contemplation. May I have the depth of heart and breadth of soul to accept that invitation to go deeper.

Taking the Contemplative Path

Recently, a guest on the News Hour said that, since we have already explored the planet Earth, space is the only remaining frontier for exploration. I truly believe in the value of space exploration. I think there is something hard-wired into most humans that has a need to *know* what is beyond the boundaries we've already discovered. But I also believe that outer space is not the last frontier. I am convinced that the exploration of *inner* space may bring about the most profound transfiguration our world has ever known. Already, thousands of people are discovering the territory within, where all beings are One. I have great hope that such deep excavations into inner reality will lead us to a breakthrough in consciousness that will help to create a better world. Right here, on planet Earth. But I believe the coming leap in consciousness must begin with you, and with me, in the silence of our own hearts.

Robert and I have discovered that the best gateway to inner space is through contemplative practice. Just as the exploration of outer space requires highly refined vehicles such as space probes and shuttles, so the exploration of inner space requires well developed vehicles such as meditation. When we speak of meditation, we are referring to *specific practices which serve to quiet the mind and consciously direct attention inward as a means of facilitating spiritual growth*. In the following pages, we plan to give clear instructions, based on our own personal experiences, for utilizing such meditative practices as centering prayer, sitting and walking meditation, and lovingkindness meditation. In addition, we'll offer some other means of soul exploration not usually found in books on contemplation.

Meditation is not, as some have suggested, a form of self-hypnosis. While hypnosis tends to *suppress* awareness, meditation is a state of *relaxed alertness* and *heightened* awareness. Scientists have demonstrated, through the use of the EEG to measure brain-wave patterns, that meditation and hypnosis are two distinctly different states. The meditative state is characterized by a slow, steady brain-wave pattern called protracted alpha, while a person in a hypnotic trance does not necessarily enter into protracted alpha at all. Her brain rhythms are more like those of any waking, working person. Self-hypnosis is a mental exercise, whereas meditation (as we've defined it) is not even an intellectual activity but rather an increase in the overall quality and depth of our total awareness. The highest states of meditative consciousness can bring an overwhelming sense of the unity of all things.

The most valuable reason for taking up a contemplative practice at *any* time in life is for developing greater spiritual awareness, and this is especially true as our years begin to dwindle. Meditation is a particularly effective form of contemplative practice because it can put one in touch with that which is greater than the small and impermanent self. A useful way to think of it is to consider that each living being is a small wave of individuality in an infinite ocean of Spirit. It is breathtakingly precious to realize that, though this single wave that I am will one day roll into shore and disappear, my true nature and being is, always has been, and always will be *ocean*. In meditation we can heighten our awareness of the great Presence that is our ultimate Source, and this is dearly comforting.

Another way that meditation can enrich the spiritual life is by helping one to see with fresh eyes. Sometimes, as I'm going about my daily routine, I catch a glimpse of the divine in something quite ordinary, such as a sun-bright aspen in autumn that seems for an instant to be made of pure golden light; or in the hovering of a tiny humming bird sipping from our feeder; or in a musical passage I've heard a hundred times that suddenly touches something sacred at my center. I have noticed that these things don't happen when I'm not being faithful to my practice. When such glimpses do come, they convince me that the divine truly inhabits all things.

Meditation can also help to enlarge the lens through which one sees the divine. Years ago I remember seeing a book entitled, *Your God Is Too Small.* Though I don't remember reading it, I think there is truth in the title. During the thirteen years I've been practicing Zen meditation, I've found my view of God becoming wider, broader, deeper, more all-inclusive, to the point that now I think of the divine as being completely boundless, existing both immanently and transcendently. Even as I write these words, I am aware of their inadequacy. Yet if you have experienced the reality of this infinite vastness, you will recognize the Presence of which I speak. These are only a few of the many ways in which meditative practices can help us to grow spiritually during our Autumn Years.

In addition to spiritual growth, scientists are discovering that there are also definite physical and psychological benefits that come with meditation. In a September 14, 2003, *New York Times* article, Stephen S. Hall reports on the results of several fascinating studies on "the biology of meditation."[8] Jon Kabat-Zinn, an emeritus professor of medicine at the University of Massachusetts Medical School, who pioneered work in the health benefits of meditation, makes it clear that meditation is becoming an acceptable field of study among scientists. Furthermore, he says "You don't have to be weird or a Buddhist or sitting on top of a mountain in India to derive benefits from this. This kind of study is in its infancy, but we're on the verge of discovering hugely fascinating things."[9]

Kabat-Zinn founded the Stress Reduction Clinic at the University of Massachusetts Medical School and has treated sixteen thousand patients and taught more than two thousand health professionals the techniques of "mindfulness meditation." Kabat-Zinn has published some fascinating studies indicating such startling facts as these: people undergoing treatment for psoriasis heal four

times as fast if they meditate; cancer patients practicing meditation had significantly better emotional outlooks than a control
group; and not only did meditation relieve symptoms in patients
with anxiety and chronic pain but also the benefits persisted up
to four years after training.[10]

Richard Davidson, a neuroscientist at the University of Wis-
consin at Madison, has been conducting a series of carefully
controlled studies on Buddhist monks in meditation. These exper-
iments are showing that "meditation may have not only emotional
effects but also distinct physiological effects," such as stress reduction, which could in turn improve immune function. In July 1977,
Davidson recruited human subjects at a small biotech company
called Promega to study the effects of meditation on American office workers. The results of the experiment were published in the
journal Psychosomatic Medicine. Among the Promega employees
who practiced meditation for two months, researchers found significant increases in activity in an area of the brain associated
with positive emotion. "Meditation ultimately left people feeling
healthier, more positive and less stressed," and this effect "persisted for at least four months after the experiment, when subjects
were tested again."[11]

Because meditation involves a process of letting go, past hurts
and traumas can be dissolved, and the thorns of such painful
emotions as old guilts can be removed. What I am about to say
is not the result of a scientific study but a personal observation.
I think meditation, because it provides practice in letting go of
mental clutter, may also help to lessen the confused thinking that
sometimes accompanies the aging process.

You and I are entering a new era. We are the children of
transition from old to new models of spiritual, medical, and psychological practices. A new kind of power is moving through our
lives. We are discovering that our true strength is our *spiritual*
strength, and that our greatest responsibility is to that. The bright,

flaming colors of the Autumn Years speak to us of a new radiance, our own inner radiance, scattering outward, planting the seeds for a new spring, lovely beyond our wildest imaginings.

Flaming Colors

I am not a botanist, but I have been told that the brilliant colors that appear in the leaves of deciduous trees during the autumn season were there all along. The chlorophyll in the leaves is what gives them their characteristic greenness in the spring and summer. As the chlorophyll recedes, the reds, yellows and oranges appear. That is a good metaphor for what can happen to us in our Autumn Years. Facets of ourselves, not manifest earlier, can gradually come to expression. In the spring and summer of our lives, our primary energies are directed toward work, family and civic responsibilities. Typically there are social expectations that go with these responsibilities and constrain what we can think, feel and do. We may not be aware of all of the constraints upon us, but they are present nonetheless. To the extent that we are aware of them, we may feel that we are not truly ourselves. Yet we accept the constraints as a necessary part of social life. In later years, as we hand over these responsibilities to others, we have the possibility of letting go of the constraints as well. When that happens we may be surprised what emerges, what hidden colors are revealed. That is one of the unexpected joys of the Autumn Years.

One of my major discoveries in these later years has been the presence of a *feminine* component in my soul. It was very important to me at an earlier time in life to establish my masculine identity, and I did so primarily through my work. As a professor of philosophy and religion, I needed highly developed analytical skills and a considerable measure of objectivity to succeed in my work. These are qualities generally associated with the masculine. By contrast, I was not encouraged to pay attention to my feelings — the more feminine side of my nature — and as a result this aspect of myself was largely neglected. When this shortcoming was brought to my attention, I honestly didn't know what to do about it. It is only recently, since I have taken up the practice of meditation, that I have begun to recognize feelings as they arise and pay attention to them. I'm still a novice at this practice, but I know that I'm a more complete person for it. The contemplative path has been for me a path to greater wholeness and self-integration.

It has involved letting go of some things. The MacArthur study, as noted earlier, tends to disparage the view that the main task of elderhood is "letting go," as if it were all about loss. To be sure there is much that we value in life that *can* continue well into the later years, especially with greater attention to healthy diet and exercise, but there are some things that we *need* to let go of in order to be more fully ourselves.

Truth be told, most of us live by a script that is in many respects outdated, constrained by roles we are no longer required to play. When I retired from college teaching, I decided to give most of my personal library to the college where I worked. It wasn't so much an expression of generosity on my part as a conscious act of letting go of a part of my life that I no longer needed. To hold onto books that I no longer had a use for would have been for me tantamount to holding onto an identity that was no longer my own. Since my retirement, I have found that I can draw upon my earlier work experience to benefit others, so it is not completely lost. But that is a matter of choice. The social expectations and rewards that went with my previous role no longer figure in my decisions, and that is quite liberating.

Retirement has freed me from many of the external restraints that prevented me from "following my bliss," to use Joseph

Campbell's famous expression, but meditation has freed me from internal hindrances that can be just as inhibiting. In my previous marriage, for instance, I often found myself acting in ways I did not approve of, ways that reminded me of what I most disliked in my father. My wife would sometimes say to me, "You're acting just like your father." I would deny it, but inwardly I knew it was true. In recent years, I've come to appreciate my father in ways I could not earlier, but I have also achieved a measure of freedom from unwanted attitudes and behaviors that I acquired from him without fully realizing it. I credit the practice of meditation with helping to create the "internal space" necessary for this kind of choice. The old patterns still show up from time to time, but when they do I can generally let go of them because my practice has prepared me for them. It has freed me to be more spontaneous, more myself in my most intimate relationships.

Falling Leaves

 We have been writing about the bright colors, the opportunities for growth, wonder, and hope that can be ours during this autumn season of our lives. Yet you and I could not have lived this long without learning the hard lesson that sadness and loss are inextricably braided in with the joys and wonders of every season of life. Even as we breathe in the glory of the breathtaking reds, oranges, and yellows of autumn trees, we can't help knowing that soon the leaves will fall and the trees will stand as bare as skeletons against a late fall sky. Just so, losses come to us all. Close friends move away, our parents and other loved ones die, our bodies begin to fail us, and we are reminded of our own mortality.

Awareness of death's cold breath at my back crashed into me like a sudden chill wind on a red and gold October day in 1995, as I was walking across the parking lot of U-Save supermarket.

Father Ford (pastor of the Episcopal Church I was attending) drove up beside me and said, "Have you heard about Carolmae?"

"What about her?"

"Cancer. Two months to live."

The Indian Summer day stopped dead, though people were walking and talking all around me, shopping carts clanging, car engines revving up. The air hung, throbbing, like a fading heartbeat, blurring everything. I could hardly breathe. I got back into the car, grocery list still in hand, and headed home. My longtime friend and prayer partner was dying? But I saw her only a week or so ago. Or was it a month or two? She *couldn't* die! We'd sat together in the silence, she and I, sharing a Presence to whom we both belonged. This couldn't be happening! And yet it was.

I spent many hours at Carolmae's bedside during the next two and a half months. Sometimes I read to her; sometimes I fed her or gave her water by holding my finger over the end of a straw submerged in a glass of water and dropping it into her mouth; sometimes I changed her. At times I cried with her. But the best times were those in which we just sat in the silence together, holding the fleeting moments, savoring them in the waning light. During the times when Carolmae slept, I pondered what it meant for me to be alive while my friend lay dying. What, I asked myself, am I going to do with my priceless remaining years?

I sat up with Carolmae the night before she died. When her daughter Linda took over at 5:00 a.m., I said goodbye to my friend, kissed her forehead, and stumbled out to my car, knowing in my heart that we'd said our last goodbye. As the great sadness washed over me, something else did, too. It was brighter than the full moon, more real than the stars. It was a deep awareness of the Presence my friend and I had shared so intimately during her lifetime. It was a once-in-sixty-years glimpse into eternity. I can never again look at the eye of the night sky without my heart falling to its knees.

I do not continue to grieve Carolmae's death. Instead of causing me to dread aging and fear death, it has made me deeply aware of the life I have *this moment,* a moment more precious than mountains and rivers. Periodically, now, life stops me and I find myself saying aloud or silently, *Amazing! I'm alive!* The words of the poet Tagore have taken on golden meaning:

> The coin of life is stamped with death
> so that what we buy will be truly precious.[12]

We invite you to join us on the contemplative path, beginning with our own personal journeys.

CHAPTER TWO

Crossing the Abyss

What can we gain by sailing to the moon if we are not able to cross the abyss that separates us from ourselves? This is the most important of all voyages of discovery. THOMAS MERTON

Elizabeth's Journey

 It's a shining black and silver night in the mid-1980s and I'm sitting in my green meditation chair in the living room of the house on 35th Street in Kearney, Nebraska. Karen and Paul, my older children, are living on their own now, and John is snugly tucked into bed. I've finished preparing my lectures for tomorrow's classes, and my husband is working late. A deep peace enters on my breath as I begin to meditate, stilling mind and body. I let my gaze fall, unfocused, onto the pool of moonlight glowing softly on the green carpet. Suddenly, out of the silence, a name rises up through the stillness within me, and some kind of soft knowing *recognizes it as my own*. How could this be? It's not my given name. Surely I must have imagined it. And yet it has seemed to come spontaneously, as if a voice were calling from somewhere other than my own mind! I try to dismiss it and go back to my meditation; but again the name comes, and again I feel the click of certain recognition. I deliberately stop trying to understand, and the name simply floats there, voicelessly, for the rest of my meditation period. It is with a deep sense of mystery that I go into the kitchen, prepare a snack for my husband, and get ready for bed.

A few evenings later, again during meditation, I seem to hear the same name being called, from just behind me and to the right. Of course no one is there. After this has happened several times in a period of two or three weeks, I begin to wonder if I'm on the far edge of sanity or if, perhaps, I'm being given a new name. I decide to tell no one, but I begin to ponder what it might mean to receive a new name. And I know that I will hold mine gently in the warmest room of my heart, for as long as it takes to understand.

What's in a Name?

I have never, in all my life, felt like a Marilyn, which is the name my parents gave me when I was born at fifteen minutes after midnight on November 1, 1930. My superstitious Granddaddy Morgan was much relieved that I'd missed Halloween, even by those few minutes. Otherwise, I might have been born a witch! However, when Sister Lucinda came swishing into Mother's hospital room to tell her that her baby had been born on All Saints' Day, Granddaddy decided I might be worth keeping after all!

I'm not sure why my parents chose the name Marilyn, except that both grandmothers and an aunt were named Mary, and Mother said she "just liked the name." It wasn't that I *disliked* the name, but from my earliest years I recognized that there was someone in me who was not Marilyn. That someone was hidden and secret and soulful, known only to the One I called God and, in surprising and unexplainable moments, to the child who went by the name of Marilyn.

Naming is an act of love. We name our children, and then we often give them pet names. Teenagers nickname their closest friends. Lovers often call each other by special names, the meaning of which is sometimes known only to the two of them.

Nineteenth-century writer George MacDonald wrote, "The true name is one which expresses the character, the nature, the being, the *meaning* of the person who bears it."[1] It is the person's own symbol, the picture of one's soul, the sign that belongs to that individual and to no one else.

I had my first glimpse of that simple but shining reality when I was a child swinging under the wisteria arbor in the back yard of my childhood home. Sometimes then, Marilyn would disappear, and Mother's tulip garden and the blue sky and singing birds were all that existed. As I grew into my teen years and beyond, I had occasional flashes of some unfathomable mystery, so much wider and deeper than the reality Marilyn knew, that I suspected there were whole worlds within and beyond me, just waiting to be discovered . . . and some unexplored identity I could not yet know.

I think most of us do get an intimate sense of the Divine, often early in life. In one brief and glowing moment, a taste is given of an unspeakable bliss, a sweet tang that disappears before it can be savored, leaving in its place a sacred hunger that turns us into seekers. In my case, the hunger led me to taste-test many different spiritual paths. And the more I tasted, the more the hunger grew. But there was so much living to do, so many things to learn, friends to make, achievements to complete; and later a husband, a home, children to love and care for, and a teaching and writing career to establish. How I longed, during those busy mid-life years, to be a "forest dweller," to have the time and a quiet place to be alone with God. I managed to *make* time in some ways I'll describe later, but it was never enough. And my secret name continued to call me to a Love beyond anything I'd ever known.

Learning to Let Go

Then the major life changes began. My three children grew up and, one after another, left home to begin their own searches, in directions different from mine. And my husband and I, whose marriage had been ailing for many years, decided to separate and finally to end our thirty-five year marriage. All changes, even the most longed for, have their melancholy; for what we leave behind us is a part of ourselves; we must die to one life before we can enter another. Though there is always pain involved in divorce, I also found an exhilarating sense of freedom and newly discovered independence. I was fifty-nine years old and ready for a fresh start and a new life. Perhaps it was time to begin my preparation for the second lifetime that the Japanese think begins at age sixty.

At this time, I was attending the Church of Dynamic Living in Kearney, Nebraska, where I heard a guest speaker named Yozan Dirk Mosig. Dr. Mosig was a professor of psychology as well as a teacher of Zen. I remember several things from that talk, but the one thing that struck me most was this. Dr. Mosig stopped in the middle of a sentence, picked up a clock, and said, "By the way, this *is* the correct time." A piece of paper covered the clock's face, and printed on the paper was the word NOW! Mosig went on to say that NOW is the only time we have to do what really matters in our lives.

What mattered most to me then, and still matters most, is spiritual growth. I asked Dr. Mosig if I might learn Zen meditation from him, and he directed me to Kearney Zen Center (which turned out to be his converted garage, carpeted and heated by a pot-bellied stove). I sat with Yozan and his students for eight years, while I also continued to attend my church and to write books on Christian Living. At that time, it felt quite inauthentic to be trying to live in two different spiritual traditions at the same time. (I would later learn how to bring the two strands together through the heart.)

I think I began practicing Zen with the hope of becoming more peaceful, and meditation did have that effect. But the unexpected part was that, in the silence of that converted garage, I began to question who I was. Sometimes answers came that surprised me. And they were by no means all pleasing discoveries. When I asked Yozan what I should do about all of these faults I was beginning to see for the first time, he said, "You don't have to do anything about them. Trying to fight them would probably be the least effective way to deal with them. Just continue to sit with your awareness of those traits and breathe into them without judging them. Changes will begin to happen. You'll see." I wasn't sure I could believe that, but I trusted him enough to follow his direction.

Who Am I, Anyway?

During the process of divorce, we placed the family home on the market and I started looking for a place of my own. Every house I looked at had something seriously wrong with it, or was in a bad location, or was too much money. Then one day my friend Cheri and I were on our way to the Post Office following our morning walk when she said, "Look! There's a sign that says FOR SALE BY OWNER. Would you like to investigate?"

"Oh, it's obviously more than I can afford," I said.

"Well, it won't hurt anything to look!"

So we knocked on the door of the house on Tabor Place — a small, quiet curved street with huge, arching trees, houses about thirty years old, and a friendly, settled look. Nine Tabor was everything I'd hoped for in a house. As we walked through, I could visualize my furniture in it; I knew where I'd put my home office, and best of all, there was a tiny room that would make a perfect meditation room. My heart was racing as I asked, with great trepidation, "What are you asking for it?" I was absolutely stunned by the answer. Cheri and I exchanged quick, startled glances. The house was only slightly more than I'd budgeted for a home!

In about two weeks, we had a reasonable offer on our 35th Street house (after nearly two years on the market), and my share of the proceeds was close to the amount I needed to make an offer on the Tabor Place home. Within a few days, papers were signed and for the first time in my life, I had a home of my own. I felt like a new woman! Suddenly the trees were greener, the sky more blue, and I was a real person. My second life had begun.

Becoming Self-Aware

We started this chapter with an epigraph from Thomas Merton about the abyss that separates us from ourselves. I have found that one cannot begin that voyage of self-discovery until she becomes *aware* of her own inauthenticities and unexamined life patterns.

Not long after my new life began, my friends Louise and George invited me for dinner one evening and included Kent,[2] a recently divorced mutual friend. A very outgoing person with a sparkling sense of humor, Kent was quite attractive and it wasn't long before I was infatuated. Other chances for dating arose, too, even as I was on the edge of age sixty (an unexpected bonus of my later years). Then one day my best friend Mona and I had lunch together and I shared some of the problems that were showing up in those relationships. She asked a penetrating question. "Do you think you might unconsciously be choosing men who are similar to your former husband?"

That night, I sat in meditation and self-examination, and I began to see that I'd been repeating some old patterns that had contributed to the failure of my marriage. Clearly, I had work to do — on myself!

At about the same time I was shopping for a dining room table. Louise asked me what furniture style I liked. The only answer I could come up with was, "I don't know!" It was another wake-up moment. In many ways, I really didn't know who I was. I realized that for most of my first six decades, I'd let others decide things for me. I seemed to have a hidden motto that said, *Whatever you do, don't "rock the boat"!*

Over the following weeks and months, I started each morning with silent meditation, asking for self-knowledge and listening for guidance. I spent time journaling daily, asking myself questions such as: *What are my priorities? How do I really want to spend the rest of my life? What might I give back to life during my autumn years?* As insights came and I tried to follow the guidance I received during prayerful contemplation, my sense of independence grew. Gradually I began to feel more like a whole person, and a few of my closest friends began calling me by my new name, *Elizabeth* — the name I had received in meditation.

Then one day I found the perfect dining-room set for my house, a cottage-style oak-and-tile table with country-blue legs and matching Windsor chairs that just felt *right*. For me, it was a very small symbol of larger inner changes occurring in many areas of my life. I was truly coming to a clearer sense of who I was. This new awareness opened me to a deeper trust in whatever life might bring.

On July 20, 1998, I legally changed my name from Marilyn to Elizabeth. In many ways, I felt I was taking a bold step toward growing into my new and (I believe) divinely given name.

Robert's Journey

If Elizabeth's journey of self-discovery could be said to have begun in a quiet moment of meditation when she was suddenly and unexpectedly given a new name, mine began with a dream, no ordinary dream but a deeply disturbing dream that came to me in the middle of the night during a meditation retreat. I was relatively new to the practice of meditation at the time, attending my third retreat in a little over a year and eager to see where this practice might lead. Several of the retreatants were gathered in the kitchen during one of the breaks, when a member of the group asked if any of the others had noticed that their dreams were more vivid during a meditation retreat than at other times. No one acknowledged having this experience, but then that night I had one of the most vivid and memorable dreams of my life.

> In the dream I am sitting behind my desk in my role as academic dean facing an angry faculty member who is sitting across from me. He is mad because I have not appointed him director of the honors program. I offer a reason for not choosing him, knowing that it is not the real reason. I am aware that he is not satisfied with my answer.

Aroused from my sleep by this disturbing dream, I had no idea what it meant. But it seemed important, so I decided to seek some help in interpreting it.

I approached a member of the group whom I knew to be a Jungian analyst and asked her if she would help me interpret my dream, and she agreed. She began with the assumption that both persons in the dream represented aspects of myself. She noted that the person sitting across from me was very powerful, so powerful that he could get me to lie. As for his wanting to be director of the honors program, that suggested he had a claim on some important part of myself. In her view, he represented the place where my core values resided. "That part of yourself," she said, "is demanding attention."

Thus began a journey of self-discovery that is still going on — a journey in which the practice of meditation has played a major role. But it was not at all obvious earlier in my life that I would ever take up the practice of meditation.

What in the World
Got You to Meditating?

I am a person who came to meditation late in life. It was not a
part of the Christian tradition in which I was raised, nor was it
included in my theological studies at one of the leading Protestant seminaries in America. As a college professor of religion, my
initial exposure to meditation came from teaching undergradu-
ates about Eastern religions. It was a purely intellectual interest
at that time: I wanted to understand how this practice func-
tioned in the context of religious traditions that were foreign to
me. Yet as I went more deeply into the subject, I became aware
that there were parallels within Christianity. My research took me
eventually to the Christian mystics who practiced a form of meditation not unlike what one finds in both Hinduism and Buddhism.
Called contemplative prayer, it is a non-verbal form of prayer in
which the person enters into a deep inward silence, standing as
it were in the presence of God, without the benefit of words or
images.

I felt personally drawn to this practice, but had no idea how to
pursue it. The most helpful book I found on the subject was written by an anonymous monk in the fourteenth century. Entitled
The Cloud of Unknowing, it includes practical suggestions for contemplative prayer, but they are not easy to follow, particularly for
someone practicing on his own. That was in the early 1970s. I
also tried yoga around the same time, but to no avail. I had no
aptitude for the more strenuous postures and had difficulty keeping up the practice. So I had nearly given up on meditation when
I left teaching for college administration in the fall of 1980.

Ten years later I was invited to join a small delegation to China,
where I had the rare opportunity to visit a famous Buddhist monastery in which monks still practice an ancient form of meditation
called Chan (Zen in Japanese). Seeing the place where the monks

meditated, I was strangely moved. Returning from the trip, I was determined to find someone who could teach me Zen meditation. I found what I was looking for in a most unlikely place, a Jesuit spirituality center in rural Louisiana, where a priest by the name of Ben Wren occasionally taught a workshop on Zen. I was somewhat wary that it might not be the "real thing," since he was after all a Catholic priest, but I was reassured by the fact that he had lived for a time in Japan and had studied with an authentic Zen master. I signed up for his advanced course, since I didn't want to wait around for the introductory course, and soon found myself plunged into thirty-to-ninety-minute periods of meditation with very little preparation.

It was a rough beginning, sitting on the floor with my legs folded in the traditional lotus position, following my breath and trying to keep my mind still. I was a total failure, but more determined than ever to pursue this practice. Two years and several retreats later (including the introductory one that I had initially passed over), I found a way to sit without excruciating pain and began the difficult process of quieting my mind. I did not practice every day, but the longer I kept at it the more natural it felt. My mind was still active, generating a relentless stream of thought whenever I tried to quiet it, but I was beginning to accept this condition as an inevitable part of the process and to experience some of the benefits that go with regular practice.

I had read about experiences of "enlightenment" that can come from meditation, mind-shattering experiences such as those the great Zen masters induced in their students, but nothing like that happened to me as I sat on my cushion. Instead I noticed that the circumstances of my life outside of the meditation room had begun to change. In the ordinary affairs of daily life, I was experiencing a greater sense of freedom and was beginning to see myself in a new way. It was then that I had the dream that awakened me to a deeper part of myself.

Preparing for Retirement

Not long after I had this "awakening dream," I went to the president of the college and told him that it was time I had a sabbatical. If I were a member of the faculty, rather than an administrator, I would have had two sabbaticals by then! I planned to go to Japan and observe first-hand religious practices I had only read about. I didn't say so at the time, but I also hoped to receive instruction in meditation from a true Zen master. My sabbatical approved, I began investigating the possibilities of taking up residence in a Zen monastery. By great good fortune I found just the right place: Sogenji, a three-hundred-year-old temple on the outskirts of Okayama (not far from Kyoto), where the abbot, an accomplished Zen teacher by the name of Shodo Harada Roshi, had assembled a community of practitioners representing over a dozen nationalities. He did not speak much English, but his assistant, an American woman who had trained with him for many years, translated for him. So his teaching was accessible to westerners in a way that most Japanese Zen teaching is not. I went there for a week-long *sesshin* (or meditation retreat), not knowing what I was getting into.

It was like being dropped into a "boot camp" for meditators, where twenty or so young people (most of them many years my junior) were training for the Zen equivalent of military combat. The day began at 4:00 a.m. with an hour of vigorous chanting followed by two hours of sitting meditation, during which every member of the community had a short meeting with the teacher. Breakfast was at seven, followed by some housekeeping chores and then more sitting until lunch at eleven. Following lunch there was a talk by the teacher and more meditation until supper. The evening meal was over by five, and by six we were back in the meditation hall. During the evening sitting period, which lasted until nine, everyone was given another opportunity to meet with

the teacher. These meetings were usually quite brief, in my case
consisting of a few words of instruction or occasionally encouragement from the teacher. The day ended shortly after nine, though
for serious practitioners there would be another hour or so of sitting outdoors before finally retiring for the night. Every day was
like that, and I struggled just to get through. Yet by the end of
the week I felt like I had been through a great cleansing process.
To my surprise I found myself thinking of coming back again!

Elizabeth speaks of a breaking-up period in her life that began
about the time she turned sixty. Something like that also happened to me about this time. I returned from Japan with the
feeling that a new life was beginning to take shape. Previously I
had not thought much about retirement, since it was still many
years off, but now I began to think that I might take early retirement. My marriage was coming to an end, and there was a
sense that I had accomplished all that I was going to accomplish
as an academic dean. There were also some things I wanted to
do that I could not even consider doing as long as I was confined
to this role. One was writing; another was deepening my practice
of meditation. I was aware that many of my colleagues did not
look forward to retirement. For them it held nothing but loss —
loss of status, loss of purpose, loss of connection to a meaningful enterprise. Some looked forward to retirement as a time for
travel and the pursuit of other interests; few, if any, saw it as a
time of new beginning. Yet that is precisely how I was coming to
regard it.

Looking back I can see that the practice of meditation was excellent preparation for retirement. That became particularly clear
to me when I heard a talk by Robert Kennedy, another Jesuit
priest who also teaches Zen meditation. He called this form of
meditation a "solvent." Over time, it will tend to dissolve even
our most cherished preconceptions and prejudices, clearing the
way for fresh experience. Spiritual growth in the Autumn Years, I

have come to see, is as much a matter of unlearning as of learning, perhaps even more so since we've had so many years to become fixed in our ways. Habits of thought and patterns of behavior which have become second nature through years of practice need to be reexamined and, in some cases, disposed of in order to make room for new growth. What makes this task so difficult is that we have a hard time getting a perspective on ourselves. The old familiar ways of thinking and acting are the lenses through which we are accustomed to viewing the world and the programs we have come to rely on to get along in the world. They may have served us well at an earlier time in our lives, but they can constitute an invisible barrier to further growth.

I am reminded of a famous Zen *koan* that goes as follows: A woman once raised a goose in a bottle, watching it grow until it was too large to pass through the neck of the bottle. Since she did not want to kill the goose or break the bottle, how was she to get it out? The master replies simply that "the goose is out." If we look at the problem objectively, as a logician might, it is absurd. The goose is either in the bottle or it is not. If it is in the bottle, there is no way to get it out without breaking the bottle; while if it is already out of the bottle, there is no problem. Zen invites us to look at the problem subjectively and see it as applying to ourselves. How many of us are trapped in a bottle we cannot see, constrained in ways we cannot seem to break free of? If meditation is a solvent, it can provide a way out of the bottle by helping us see the constraints for what they are — something of our own making and therefore of our own unmaking if we so choose.

Anyway that is how meditation worked for me. It put me in touch with a larger and deeper aspect of myself and cleared an inner space from which to view the world with new eyes. It enabled me, at age sixty-two to consciously leave one life and enter another, without knowing exactly where that new life might lead.

Companions on the Way

Elizabeth and I began our late-life journeys of self-discovery in-dependently. Only after we were well on the way did our paths converge. You may call it synchronicity or providence or just good fortune, but we seem to have found each other at just the right time. We are frequently asked, "How did you two get together?" And we generally reply, "To begin with, we are cousins." Then we wait to see the response. Some people are a bit uncomfortable with the idea of cousins marrying. In fact, we have been asked if it is illegal. The answer is that in some states it is, but not in Colorado, where we live. We don't know why it would be illegal, especially for couples past the childbearing age, but it may be one of those taboos that lingers on long after it has served its purpose. In any case, we consider it an advantage. Having some genes in common no doubt makes us more compatible, but more impor-tant, we feel, are the values we share and the family memories we have in common because we are cousins.

We did not see a lot of each other when we were growing up, but our mothers were sisters and their families did occasionally get together. Vacations in Colorado, where our grandparents owned cabins, were especially meaningful to us when we were young. But there was a long period of time when we hardly saw each other: the early and middle adult years when we were heavily involved with our own families and careers. So when we got together briefly in December 1996, we had some catching up to do.

That fall was a major turning point in my life. I notified the college that I would be retiring at the end of the academic year, received approval to spend the next fall at the monastery in Japan where I had visited two years earlier, and applied for a resident fellowship at a research institute in Minnesota for the following spring. My immediate future seemed fairly clear at that point, but I was in for a surprise. Returning from Colorado, where I'd spent

Christmas with my daughter, I stopped off in Nebraska to visit my cousin, whom I hadn't seen in many years. I knew that we had similar interests. What I didn't know was that we were on the same spiritual path.

 The relationships I had after my divorce were unsatisfying to me, mainly because the one thing I wanted more than anything else was a close spiritual companion. After eight years as a single woman, I had decided that I was not going to meet such a man. I had also decided I rather liked being independent and living alone. So when my cousin Robert visited, I told him I had decided not to marry again.

In all the years I'd known Robert, I'd felt a special affinity with him among my cousins. Now here he was, sitting across from me at my dining-room table, and we were getting reacquainted. The conversation went something like this:

ELIZABETH: "So, what have you been doing lately?"

ROBERT: "Well, I've been practicing a little Zen."

ELIZABETH: "Really?!"

ROBERT: "What have *you* been doing?"

ELIZABETH: "Well, I've been practicing some Zen."

Of course we laughed, but for some reason, I don't think either of us was surprised. We sat together that evening in my little meditation room with its altar bearing the cross of Christ, candles, and incense, and with our sitting time marked by my Japanese Zen bell. It all felt so *right.*

I wouldn't really say I *fell* in love. It was more an *awakening* into love that took root in me and grew slowly. It was composed of small memories of such moments as the December night when Robert first sat in my kitchen and read to me and we laughed away our reserve; the sweet-sad loneliness I felt when, after having sat in meditation with him, I now sat alone; love letters from across the sea; two-hour phone calls; long talks about life and death and matters of the heart and soul; and finally, that magical night when he reached across the table at Kearney's best restaurant, took my hands in his and said, "When the time is right, will you marry me?"

My answer then came quickly, from a deeply rooted certainty. "Yes. Oh yes!"

I had found my spiritual companion, and our marriage has become the treasure of my Autumn Years.

On New Year's Day, 1999, in the company of our children and grandchildren, we became husband and wife. Our separate paths had merged into one. It would not be the conventional path marked out by our religious tradition, but one of our own making, incorporating contemplative practices from various traditions, and that was all right. We were ready to walk together as interfaith pilgrims in a spiritual adventure filled with discovery and grace.

CHAPTER THREE

Interfaith Pilgrims

Say not, "I have found the truth," but rather, "I have found a truth."　　　　　　　　　　　　　　　KAHLIL GIBRAN

 Unlike Robert, who discovered the contemplative path later in life, I think I've been in love with something like contemplation since I was a child. Though I had playmates, I was quite young when I discovered the joy of solitude. How I cherished spending an hour or more sitting alone in my brother's tree house, watching the clouds, listening to the birds, and silently "talking to God." It seemed, then, that God was my soul friend, the One I could talk with honestly about whatever was on my mind, the Companion who would never leave me. As I look back on it now, I think these and other direct spiritual experiences were more precious to me than all the memorized prayers, Bible stories, and creeds I learned in Sunday School.

I'm a cradle Episcopalian and I've loved my church, especially the liturgy and the Holy Eucharist, all my life. Even more, I've loved my private prayer times. Still, I can't remember a time when I could honestly say that Christianity was the *only* path to God. My beliefs, like those of most of us, came to me secondhand, from my parents, teachers, and my church. I realized at some point that, *unless I could let <u>doubt</u> in enough to examine my beliefs, my faith could never truly be my own.* That was when I began reading about other religious traditions and trying on some of their practices. It was something I had to do in order to get out of the procrustean bed and stretch my soul. To my surprise, none of these explorations diminished my faith in that which is beyond naming. Instead, the adventure actually broadened and enriched and made more authentic the Truth that I have now come to know as my own.

A Convergence of Traditions

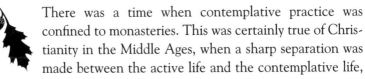There was a time when contemplative practice was confined to monasteries. This was certainly true of Christianity in the Middle Ages, when a sharp separation was made between the active life and the contemplative life, but it has been the case throughout most of Western history. To pursue a contemplative life, it was supposed, one must renounce the world, take vows of celibacy and poverty, and devote oneself exclusively to prayer. Monasteries existed to support this kind of life. While it was not for everyone, for those who had this calling it was considered the "better way." Contemplative practice, it was felt, brought one closer to God.

The Protestant Reformation, along with the rise of secularism, challenged this assumption. During the modern period, beginning in the early seventeenth century, the active life came to be valued above the contemplative, even among the religious. By the time I entered seminary, such a path was not even considered a viable option. Theological students of my generation wanted to be out in the world, engaged in the great movements of social change. We read Dietrich Bonhoeffer, took part in civil rights marches, and joined the opposition to the nuclear arms race and eventually the Vietnam War. We took up the cause of feminism and were early proponents of environmentalism. The contemplative life would have seemed to us "socially irresponsible."

Yet even at the height of the social activism of the 1960s, a sea change was taking place. A number of young people, mainly on the West coast, had discovered the meditative traditions of Asia. Some were even traveling to India, Burma, and Japan in order to train with Hindu and Buddhist teachers. They were challenging the prevailing view that the active life is the only life worth pursuing by looking outside of Western culture for an alternative. About the same time, a similar development was occurring within the Catholic Church inspired by the writings of Thomas Merton. He was the kind of person who might have been a social activist, but chose instead to enter a monastery in order to pursue the contemplative path. He made it his task to recover the contemplative tradition within Christianity, not only for himself but for others living outside of the monastery. His writings awakened an interest in contemplation that had been largely dormant for several hundred years and presented it as a possibility for everyone. Moreover, he found through his readings an affinity with the meditative practices of Asia, particularly Zen. So from the outset the modern-day contemplative movement has brought together practices from various religious traditions.

There are many varieties of contemplative practice, even within a single religious tradition such as Buddhism. Colorado Springs is the city nearest to the village where Elizabeth and I live. It is in many ways a very conservative city with a strong military presence and an active evangelical community. Yet one can find here groups practicing three distinct forms of Buddhist meditation: Vipassana, Tibetan, and Zen. To the outsider they might seem the same, but each tradition has a long history and its own particular form of practice. That could also be said for the Christian contemplative tradition, which had its beginning with the Desert Fathers, who were for the most part hermits, but soon spread to Europe through the formation of monastic communities, which in turn formed their own traditions and developed their own practices. While these various practices — Buddhist and Christian — developed for the most part independently, in our day they coexist, often in close proximity, and are coming to have a distinct influence on one another.

Thomas Keating is an example of a spiritual leader who has encouraged this interaction. As the abbot of a Benedictine monastery in Spencer, Massachusetts, during the 1960s and well into the 1970s, he participated in the monastic reform movement inspired by the Second Vatican Council. He was charged with recovering the original impetus for his religious order, and this took him back to contemplative practice. But he did not want to limit the practice to monks; he wanted to reach out to those outside of the order who had expressed a need for spiritual direction. He was especially touched by reports of young people traveling to Asia in order to find a spiritual practice they felt was lacking in their own religious tradition. So he established contact with a Buddhist monastery in the vicinity and entered into conversation with the monks in residence there. Before long they were visiting each other's communities and taking part in each other's religious practices. They found that in spite of their differences, which were not insignificant, there was an underlying spirit that united them. It was their contemplative practice that took them to this place of unity — beyond doctrine and liturgy, beyond words and images.

Practicing Within Two Traditions

I have personally experienced this convergence of traditions. I spent the year following my retirement as a guest in two quite different religious communities. In the fall of 1997, I took up residence at Sogenji, the Japanese Zen Buddhist monastery that I'd visited three years earlier. I stayed in their guest house, but otherwise participated fully in the life of the monks. For three months I lived on a diet consisting mainly of rice, soup, fruit and vegetables. I rose early every morning to chant sutras, took my turn at the various tasks required to maintain the community, from sweeping paths to cleaning toilets, sat with the monks in meditation for a minimum of five hours a day (ten to twelve hours during the week-long intensive retreats which took place once or twice a month), and took long walks when I was not otherwise occupied.

My chief fear was the cold. Japanese monasteries do not have central heating; in fact most of the time there is no heating at all. On my first visit, in early October, the temperature had dropped suddenly from the mid-seventies to the low forties, and I was caught totally unprepared. This time I came loaded with Polartec, but I wasn't sure it would be enough to get me through the fall. I wanted to stay through December 8 in order to experience Rohatsu, the traditional date of Buddha's enlightenment and the high point of the year for Zen practitioners. On this date they sit through the night in the hope of duplicating Buddha's experience. I had no expectation of enlightenment, but did want to take part in this event. Knowing how cold it could get that time of year, I wasn't sure I could do it.

I found that I was able to adjust to the long periods of sitting and settle into the rhythm of monastic life. I carefully rationed my layers of warm clothes to make sure that I would have enough protection from the cold to get me through Rohatsu. At one point I told Harada Roshi that I thought I could go a whole year; I was really enjoying the life of a Zen monk. Then came the week leading up to Rohatsu. The schedule was accelerating with longer daily sits and a more austere diet, but worst of all the weather was getting much colder. I had exhausted my supply of warm clothes and now faced the prospect of going into the coldest night of the year without extra protection. Late in the evening of Rohatsu, while sitting on the porch waiting my turn to meet with the teacher, I considered running back to my room and looking for something more to put on, anything that might help me get through the night. I was desperate! But then the thought came to me: "Why are you so afraid of the cold? What if you are miserable for a few hours? You aren't going to die of the cold." In that moment the fear vanished and I realized that it was *fear* of the cold rather than the cold itself that was causing me to suffer. For the rest of the night, I was fine. I didn't experience the "great awakening" that Buddha experienced, but I had my own breakthrough.

Following my three-month stay at the Zen monastery, I took up residence for the next five months at the Institute for Ecumenical and Cultural Research in Collegeville, Minnesota. Readers of Kathleen Norris's *Cloister Walk* will be familiar with this remarkable place which, because of its affiliation with both St. John's University and a nearby Benedictine abbey, is able to offer an unparalleled opportunity for scholarly research within a monastic setting. As one of seven resident scholars, I lived in a guest house on the outskirts of the campus not far from the abbey. Although there was no requirement to participate in the life of the monks, we were permitted to join them for morning, noon and evening religious services. I took advantage of this opportunity whenever I could.

Most days began with a half-mile walk to the abbey church, where I sat in the choir, sang hymns, chanted psalms and recited prayers with the monks before going to the library to work. Aware that only a short time before I had been chanting sutras with Buddhist monks, I felt a wonderful convergence of religious traditions. The words were different, but the spirit of reverence and inner peace was much the same. I felt a part of something much larger than myself, a mysterious oneness with what can only be called *Ultimate Reality*. Words fail to do justice to the experience.

I had thought I might feel a tension between these two religious traditions once I entered deeply into them, but that was not the case. My Zen practice, if anything, opened me to the deeper meaning of Christian contemplative writings, such as the psalms. I had gone about as far as I could go with an intellectual understanding of the Christian faith; what I needed was a more experiential understanding. Meditation provided that extra dimension. My year as a guest in these two monastic communities gave me a platform on which to construct my own version of the contemplative life. I would not exchange that year for any other in my life; yet I am not a monk. I have chosen, together with my spiritual companion, to make my own way in the world — drawing on these two spiritual traditions, and any other that might come to hand, and subtly weaving them together.

A Winding Path

 The convergence of traditions was clear cut for Robert. For me, the process came more gradually and the route was indirect. Though my church fed the devotional aspect of my faith, there was still a longing within me for a spiritual practice that would put me in direct contact with the deep inner truth that underlies all belief systems. The lack of a practicing contemplative group within my church led me to become a seeker, an *interfaith pilgrim* in search of a path that might fulfill the longing that had been within me always.

In 1973, I heard a television interview with a woman named Anita, who was a teacher of Transcendental Meditation. What I noticed about her was that she seemed to radiate a deep, serene presence, as though she were connected to something strong and solid within. The interviewer asked her if she'd always been that way, and her reply was that her life had been extremely chaotic in many ways, both externally and internally, and that was what drew her to the practice of meditation. *I wanted what Anita had!*

A few days later, I signed up for training in the practice of TM, a form of meditation derived from the Hindu religion, in which the practitioner uses the repetition of a *mantra* (a one-syllable word or short phrase) to become centered. It's not necessary to adopt a new belief system or discard one's current beliefs to practice TM. It was my first experience with a traditional contemplative practice, and I found it quite rewarding. To my surprise, *it deepened and enriched my Christian practice.* In addition, it provided me with a way to cope with stress during the time that I was teaching college English, caring for a family of six, and writing my first two books.

During that time, I developed a strong desire to seek out the contemplative dimension in my own tradition and to introduce other Christians to meditation, so I began reading the mystics such as St. John of the Cross, St. Teresa of Avila, and such books as *The Cloud of Unknowing*, *Poustinia*, and *The Way of a Pilgrim.* I searched the Bible for references to contemplative practices in order to reassure myself and others that there was a basis for meditation within our own Scriptures. Then I wrote my book *Beyond TM: A Practical Guide to the Lost Traditions of Christian Meditation.*[1]

Within a few weeks after publication of an excerpt from the book in a national magazine, the mail started pouring in. Though 90 percent of it was positive, I was shocked to find that the other 10 percent was very negative! Some people wrote such things as "Don't you realize that meditation is of the devil?" Or "This is very dangerous! You are encouraging people to open themselves to all the forces of evil!" Or "These are Eastern practices! How dare you present them in the context of a book on Christianity!" I had no idea that there was such fearfulness around the subject of meditation/contemplation!

Of course, that was over twenty years ago and attitudes have changed somewhat. Many Christians have taken up practices such as Zen, Yoga, and Transcendental Meditation without throwing away their Christian faith. I mention these negative reactions only because I know that such fearful attitudes still exist among some of the more literal-minded Christian denominations. It is our hope that readers will take from this book on contemplation in the Autumn Years the ideas that are fitting for them and leave the rest. We are most certainly not implying that the path we have chosen is right for everyone.

Something More

I continued to practice Transcendental Meditation more or less regularly for seventeen years. Still, the longing that originally drew me to it continued to urge me on to something more. At that time I discovered a Catholic monastery in Hastings, Nebraska,[2] about an hour's drive from my home, where I took workshops in centering prayer, and later co-led retreats with Father Joseph Smerke. Centering prayer is the form of contemplative practice taught by Father Thomas Keating, who now resides in Snowmass, Colorado, and directs a worldwide organization called Contemplative Outreach. It is a practice that uses a *sacred word* as a focus to bring the wandering mind back to God during the practice of meditation.

The Crosier Monastery also offered me silence and solitude in the form of the *Poustinia,* a one-room hermitage cottage nestled among the tall pines at the far edge of the property. For several years, I regularly spent twenty-four-hour periods there each month. I knew that in this setting there would be no interruptions, no meetings, no lesson plans or meals to prepare, no laundry or ironing to do. My possessions there consisted of a freshly-baked loaf of nutritious bread and a thermos of water, given to me by Father Joe, my Bible, a notebook, cushions, and my sleeping bag.

I loved the reflection of the kerosene lantern glow on the wash basin and pitcher, the crackling of the fire in the little wood-burning stove, the open Bible on the desk in front of the window. In the distance I could hear a train whistle, children playing, leaves blowing. Yet there was a silence greater than any of the sounds, an inner silence that sometimes goes with me, even now. As soon as I'd walk through the hermitage door, whatever emotional load I'd been carrying in with me would begin to slip away. I spent my time there praying, pondering God's healing presence, and just being present in love, with the indwelling divine. I came to know an inner Being who was both companion and guide to me, and I always went away nourished, in touch with God and myself, made whole.

During this time of intense practice of contemplative prayer in the Christian tradition, I was introduced to Zen meditation and began sitting regularly with my teacher, Yozan Dirk Mosig, and his other students. As I mentioned earlier, combining the two practices created some feelings of inauthenticity within me, giving rise to something of a spiritual crisis.

This was the point in my spiritual journey at which Robert came into my life. We discovered, rather quickly, that we were on a similar spiritual path. We had each found our way to Zen separately, coming to it from strong Christian roots. The first evening we were together, I talked with him about my difficulty in integrating the two traditions. He had already dealt with some of the issues I was struggling with and explained how they had come together for him. This helped me to see that it was possible to practice Zen meditation without betraying my Christian faith.

Complementarity

 When Elizabeth asked me how I could reconcile practicing within two religions as different as Buddhism and Christianity, my first response was that Christianity is not without its own *internal* differences, some of which are as difficult to reconcile as those which separate Buddhists from Christians. Protestants and Catholics, after all, have been at odds for over five hundred years, while the Eastern Orthodox Church and the Roman Catholic Church have followed separate paths for over a thousand years. Only recently have the diverse branches of Christianity begun to reestablish communion with one another, and still major differences of belief and practice persist. Buddhism has a similar, if somewhat less acrimonious history, spawning over the course of twenty-five hundred years many variations and permutations. So if people are going to practice only with those who believe and act as they do, they will find themselves cut off from most of the world's spiritual practitioners.

I prefer to follow the lead of persons like the Catholic Thomas Merton and the Buddhist Thich Nhat Hanh, who discovered a deep spiritual kinship in spite of their religious differences.[3] Because their contemplative/meditative practices took them to a place beyond words and images, they could see that the words and images we use to speak of the Great Mystery are always incomplete and inadequate. I am reminded of the story of the four blind men feeling an elephant and each coming up with a different idea of what kind of animal it is. The one who has hold of the trunk thinks it is a snake, the one touching a leg supposes it is a tree, the one who grasps its tail is sure it is a rope, while the one feeling its ear thinks it must be like a fan. We tend to think that our different interpretations of Ultimate Reality must be contradictory, when they could just as well be complementary. As long as we do not insist that our own beliefs are the only true beliefs, we should be able to practice with one another and even learn from one another.

If you look deeply into the world's great religions, and do not get caught up in their cultural differences, I believe you will find that they contain many of the same elements expressed in different ways. Buddhists, for instance, tend to speak of Ultimate Reality in more impersonal terms than Christians; yet you can find in the writings of some Christians, especially the mystics, a similar way of speaking about God. Christians, on the other hand, are inclined to look upon Eastern religions, such as Buddhism, as excessively "quietist," indifferent to issues of social justice; yet in our own day we have seen the emergence in these very religions of a form of "engaged spirituality" every bit as activist as anything found in the West. By practicing together, we may find that it is possible to develop a more whole and integrated faith within our own tradition. We may also find that we are comfortable practicing within more than one tradition, that *we do not have to choose.*

A Longing for the Devotional

 Following a long-distance courtship, Robert and I were married and spent our wedding trip at Plum Village in the south of France, with the community of the Vietnamese Buddhist monk Thich Nhat Hanh. Both of us had read many books by this gentle mannered, solidly grounded teacher of mindfulness meditation. During our two weeks of practice there, Nhat Hanh (or Thay, as he is called by his followers) gave talks twice a week. In one of those addresses, he made the statement, "You don't have to become a Buddhist to practice Zen meditation. Go back to your own tradition and look deeply into it. You'll find the same thing imbedded in the roots of your own religion."

Yes! I knew it was true, from my readings of Christian mystics. Yet I also felt there was something in my Christian faith that seemed lacking in Zen. Though there were devotional practices in Zen (bowing, chanting, candle lighting, incense), there seemed to be no *receiver* of that devotion. In some forms of Buddhism, the Buddha, and sometimes other deities as well, are worshipped, but this is not true of Zen. Instead, there is an all-inclusive boundlessness that is sometimes called emptiness. For me, it is clear that

Buddha was a man, not a God, but how could I feel devotional about something as impersonal as boundlessness?

I have held that question for a long time, and gradually, petal by petal, a beautiful flower has begun to open in the heart of my practice. I've come to know the divine, not as a totally transcendent being on high, *nor* as an impersonal, external unknowable, but as the Great Mystery that dwells within me as the Beloved *and* as that infinite boundlessness that is inseparable from mountains and rivers and all living beings, and that includes love and suffering, compassion, hope and grace. Now when I bow before the Zen altar, it is a devotional practice because I am bowing to the indwelling Beloved *and* the infinite Boundlessness within all beings.

Recently, as I walked into Shove Chapel on the Colorado College campus where we practice with our Zen group, I was overcome by the beauty of the stained glass, touched by the Christian symbols of the main altar, and stirred by echoes of love from my long-time church home. At the same time, I felt a great love for what was represented by our Zen altar, with its Buddha statue, incense, candle and flowers. There they were, side by side, two altars surrounded by a great and mystical silence so all-encompassing that something inside of me knelt. And when I looked within, I found a most unusual flower blooming near the center of my chest. Was it a rose? Was it a lotus? Then I saw that it had two stems closely bonded together. It was both.

What I've learned in my journeying so far is that one must find her own way through the forest of religious traditions, and that for some of us, the most authentic way combines elements from more than one path. Like Robert, I've discovered that it's possible to practice Zen meditation without abandoning my Christian faith. I continue to value the liturgy and Holy Eucharist of the Episcopal Church, write for a major Christian publication, and practice centering prayer in addition to my Zen meditation. Clearly, it's the contemplative dimension in both traditions that binds them together in my soul. Perhaps your own exploration will also lead you to a meeting place of two religious traditions.

Dual Citizenship

Jenny, my daughter by my previous marriage, was born in England of American parents, so she has dual citizenship. She is both American and British. Elizabeth and I consider ourselves "dual citizens" in respect to our religious identity. We have not given up one identity in order to take on another, but rather participate freely in both traditions. It is our contemplative practice that is the common denominator. At a time in our lives when we are drawn to the practice of contemplation, there are many resources at our disposal and many models for the kind of creative interweaving of traditions we find appealing.

We would like to introduce you to some of these resources and the ways we have found to integrate them.

CHAPTER FOUR

Finding Your Own Practice

Submit to a daily practice.
Your loyalty to that
Is a ring on the door.
Keep knocking, and the joy inside
Will eventually open a window
And look out to see who's there.

                    JELALUDDIN RUMI

My father was an old-fashioned, twenty-four-hour-a-day doctor who made house calls to farm homes in snow storms in the middle of the night. He was usually up at 7:00 a.m. for surgery and office hours lasted until there were no more patients waiting — which was often seven or eight in the evening. But he always came home at noon, and before eating he'd go into the sunroom and close the door for a half hour of quiet time alone. I knew it was this time of stillness and quiet renewal that gave him the strength to endure the long hours and that kept alive the positive outlook that was so much a part of his character.

I used to ask my dad, "What do you *do* during that time?"

His answer: "I just sit still, clear my mind, and get in tune with the Infinite."

When I'd ask him how he did this, he'd say, "Well, I can't really say. Everyone has to find his own way." That answer didn't really satisfy me, but it wasn't until I was a young married woman with small children that I began, in earnest, to search for my own way.

I think having a spiritual practice is like creating a beautiful inner garden. Attending church every Sunday is a precious spiritual practice. That's where the seeds are planted. But unless we feed and weed and water regularly, the seeds are not likely to grow into beautiful plants.

Robert and I have found that contemplative practice feeds our souls in much the same way that a vegetable garden feeds our bodies, and like a beautiful flower garden, the regular practice of meditation brings a quiet beauty into our lives. This seems especially valuable at the Autumn Years stage of life, when we are beginning to be less able to do the active things we formerly did. Sometimes people in this age group feel their lives are drying up, shriveling. When these feelings arise, how refreshing it is to have a "place" to go for inner nourishment and the cultivation of spiritual beauty.

For this reason, we are going to write at some length about four kinds of traditional meditation practice: sitting meditation, centering prayer, walking meditation, and lovingkindness meditation. We suggest that you try each of them for at least a couple of weeks, and then narrow down to one (or possibly two) types that feel particularly suited to your soul. We'll also offer a brief discussion of some other practices that you might decide to use as adjuncts to your primary form(s) of meditation.

Sitting Meditation

Sometime during the 1960s, or perhaps it was the 1970s, I recall seeing a bumper sticker that read "Don't just do something, sit there." It was a delightful rebuke to the characteristically American disposition to *do* something, anything! To "just sit" seemed irresponsible, yet for a growing number of Americans, even then, sitting meditation was coming to have a distinct appeal. It offered a counterbalance to the frenetic activism that seemed to consume people, a path to inner peace at a time of great social upheaval. Since there were no ready examples of this kind of practice in most of our religious traditions, those who wanted to practice sitting meditation were obliged to look elsewhere. The Eastern religions, notably Hinduism and Buddhism, offered the best resource. They had been perfecting this practice for many hundreds, indeed thousands of years.

In the course of this long history, many versions of the practice have evolved. I was personally drawn to Zen meditation, in large part because of its simplicity. The form of sitting meditation that I was taught, first by a Jesuit priest and later by a Japanese Zen master, focuses on the breath. Breathing, according to this tradition, is the key to stilling and concentrating the mind. It is what puts one in touch with one's deepest spiritual nature. That might seem surprising, since nothing is so ordinary and taken for granted as breath. We breathe continuously, usually without thinking. If we are tired or anxious, we may notice that our breath has become shallow, strained or irregular, but for the most part we do not notice our breath. In sitting meditation of the sort I was taught, you are asked to pay specific attention to your breath.

But first you need to be properly seated. Sitting meditation begins with establishing a good sitting position. In Japan and most Asian cultures that means sitting on a cushion on the floor. As one of my teachers who had lived for many years in Japan said, the Japanese are a people of the floor. They sit on the floor for conversation and often eat their meals from tables barely a foot off of the floor. Even their beds are typically without a frame, simply a futon spread out on the floor at night and taken up during the day. So for them sitting on the floor is natural, whereas for us it is not. I eventually learned to sit on a cushion on the floor, but it was extremely difficult. Even then I did not succeed in sitting cross-legged in the traditional lotus position. Elizabeth can do that, but I'm simply not flexible enough. For Westerners taking up meditation in the Autumn Years, it is not reasonable to expect them to sit on the floor. Moreover, it is not necessary. A chair will do just as well. In fact, everywhere I have practiced sitting meditation, even in Japan, there has been someone sitting on a chair.

The important thing is that you sit with your back straight. A slouch will not do. There are several reasons for this, but the main one is that you cannot sit still very long in a slouch. You will soon become uncomfortable and want to move around. If the object of sitting meditation is to still the mind, you must first still the body. Sitting with your back straight is the best way to keep still. Believe me, you can sit perfectly still for long periods of time if your back is straight. A straight back is also needed for deep, steady breathing. It opens a pathway for the breath to flow freely from the abdomen through the lungs and out the nostrils. You do not need to sit in a rigid posture — in fact, you want to be relaxed — but you should eliminate as much as possible the curvature in your lower back.

Sitting in a kneeling position on the floor as I do, I find that pushing forward with my pelvis and raising my chest helps to keep my back straight. If you decide to sit in a chair, be sure that it is a straight chair and that your feet are flat on the floor. Sitting on a small cushion placed at the back of the chair seat, so that the hips are elevated above the knees, can help to align the back. If you're not very tall, it also helps to place another cushion or thick mat on the floor so that your feet rest comfortably without distorting your posture. Try different ways of sitting until you find one that is comfortable and relaxing. No one way is right for everyone. Whatever works for you is fine.

When I went to Japan the first time, I knew that I would be in for long periods of sitting and thought I might need help with my sitting posture, which was certainly not the best. What I found instead was that my teacher ignored my posture and focused exclusively on my breathing. In our very first interview he asked me to breathe for him, meaning he wanted to *hear* my breath. I managed somehow to breathe loudly enough for him to hear, but my breath was shallow and halting. I struggled to get out as much air as I could, but it felt pretty pitiful. He did not seem overly concerned, however, and followed my meager effort with a demonstration of his own long, slow, deep breath. Then he told me that my training would not be about acquiring a particular technique, but rather "returning to my original breath."

In the days that followed I did more sitting than I had ever done in my life, approximately ten hours a day on the cushion, with breaks for meals, housekeeping chores, a talk by the teacher and some sleep (no more than six hours a night). I struggled to get through periods of sitting that could last for several hours with short periodic walking or stretching breaks. On the very last day, after sitting with pain in my back and legs most of the time, I suddenly realized that the pain was gone. Then, to my great surprise, my breathing changed. It became smooth and regular, deeper than I had ever known. I realized that I had found my *original breath.* I'd spent my whole life, it seemed, acquiring knowledge and expertise, impressing people with my mastery of this and that, yet here I was back at the very beginning, learning to breathe — of all things! I told the teacher's assistant that I felt as though I had completed a course in "remedial breathing."

There are techniques you can use to focus attention on your breath. One of these techniques is counting. You might try counting to ten, one count for each in-breath and each out-breath, repeating the process until your mind is quiet and your attention fully concentrated on your breath. That may sound easy, but you will find that you soon lose count. Your mind will wander and you'll forget where you were in your counting. Then you'll have to start over: one, two, three, etc. You can vary the routine by just counting to two (one on the in-breath, two on the out-breath) or by merely repeating the word "one" to yourself every time you exhale. What I was taught to do is to visualize a column of air rising slowly from my abdomen as I exhale and descending slowly from the top of my head as I inhale. Whichever method you use, it helps to concentrate on the *exhalation*. If you exhale as fully and deeply as you can, you will find that the inhalation takes care of itself.

Attending to the breath, I find, does help to quiet the mind. It may not seem so at first, since the mind can be extremely active, particularly when you have nothing to do but sit. (You'll be surprised what thoughts come up, things you hadn't thought of in years, more often than not things you don't want to think about!) Paying attention to your breath does not put an end to thought, but it can be a way of breaking the relentless chain of associations that invariably arise, often without your realizing it. By following your breath all of the way to the end, exhausting your lungs as fully as possible, you interrupt this process of association and free your mind, if only momentarily, for something else. In time you will observe the thought process slowing down, until finally a deep stillness enters into your consciousness. I have sometimes wondered if that is not what the apostle Paul had in mind when he referred to "the peace that passes understanding."

How long, you may ask, should I sit at any one time? To begin with, you will probably not want to sit for more than ten or fifteen minutes at a stretch. But if you do that every day, before long you will find yourselves sitting twenty or thirty minutes at a time. It is generally recommended that a person starting out try to sit twice a day for short periods of time (such as a half hour in the morning and a half hour in the early evening), rather than sit less regularly for longer periods of time. But just as there are many forms of sitting meditation, there are many ideas about how best to maintain this practice. You will have to decide what is best for you. Yet whatever form you take up and for however long you practice it, I believe you will find that it makes a profound difference in the quality of your life. It certainly has for me.

Centering Prayer

 Another form of sitting meditation that may be more to the liking of deeply devoted Christians is centering prayer. I have found that it brings me back, again and again, to the sacred center of my being, where the Divine dwells within me.

Even during the Autumn Years, I think many of us live in a world whirling with activity, or we deliberately fill up our time to the extent that we lose awareness of our true Center. Here's an image that has helped me. When my son John was in elementary school, he walked out the front door one morning on his way to school. A few seconds later he was back. "Mom! Come quick!" I hurried outside and saw the most beautiful spider web I'd ever seen. The sun was shining on it in just the right way to create a rainbow of colors. Then John told me something he'd learned in school. He said that spiders walk only on the spokes of the web. That's because the circular parts are sticky in order to trap the spider's bug meals. So what the resident spider does when she wants to move to another part of the web is to walk outward on a spoke and then, before moving on, she always goes back to the center. *That's what's wrong in my life,* I thought. *I'm going around in circles without taking time to return to my center between tasks.* I have found that centering prayer is a precious way of returning to that inner center where Love dwells. In the mid-1980s, I was invited to attend a two-week workshop on contemplative prayer at the Crosier Monastery in Hastings, Nebraska. Led by my good friend Father Joe Smerke, it was built around centering prayer, as developed by Father Thomas Keating. What I discovered at the workshop was that centering prayer is really quite similar to some of the meditation techniques I'd already been practicing and writing about. For readers who are uncomfortable using meditative practices derived from Eastern traditions, this may be a just-right alternative. I find it to be a very heart-centered form of meditation that feeds the devotional aspect of my spirituality. There's a lovely passage in the Song of Songs that expresses this:

> With great delight I sat in his shadow
> and his fruit was sweet to my taste
> He brought me to the banqueting house,
> And his banner over me was love.[1]

This is exactly what my experience in centering prayer has been for me — a time to sit in the shade of the Divine and bask in that Love.

When I teach or practice centering prayer, I like to begin with a brief period of stretching followed by three long, slow, deep breaths. This relaxes the body and makes it easier to sit still during the meditation period. It's also good to follow the instructions Robert has given for sitting comfortably in a chair. Centering prayer is usually practiced with the eyes closed, but if you find yourself becoming sleepy, I'd suggest you open your eyes slightly and cast them downward toward the floor, letting them go out of focus.

It's important to realize that, in centering prayer we aren't trying to reach out to an external Being but to get in touch with the Divine Light that is already at the center of our being. So, how do you do this type of prayer? The answer is you don't *do* it. You let it happen to you. As Father Joe used to say, "God prays you."

Centering prayer involves the silent repetition of a "sacred word" so the first step is to ask for your own sacred word. Many people like to use one of the names of God or simply the word Love. The anonymous author of *The Cloud of Unknowing* suggests that a one-syllable word such as love, joy, or peace is best. Father

Keating believes it's best to use a word that doesn't have special personal meaning for you, so that your mind won't wander off following the associations you have about the word. Sometimes a sacred word arises spontaneously, but if this doesn't happen, it's perfectly acceptable just to choose a word that feels right to you at the heart. *Always let your heart be your guide.* When you have your sacred word, you are ready to begin.

Now just sit quietly focusing your attention at the heart. Sometimes I place my hand over my heart because it helps me to hold my attention there. Then just wait patiently for the previously chosen sacred word to arise. Don't try to force it, but just begin to repeat the word gently and silently into the stillness of your heart/mind, as often as it feels natural to you. It is not necessary to coordinate the word with your breathing. That may happen naturally or it may not, but it is counterproductive to make a point of it.

Within a very short time, you will notice that your mind has started to wander. That's perfectly natural. When you notice that a stray thought has entered your mind, just gently bring your attention back by silently returning to your sacred word. Be gentle with yourself. Don't *fight* thoughts. When they intrude, simply notice them and return to your sacred word. You will no doubt have to do this many times, but the beautiful thing about this is that, each time you let go of a thought and return to your sacred word, you're releasing some of your accumulated inner tension. You're also practicing letting go, which can carry over into your daily life in beautiful ways. I like to think of it as a *surrender into tranquility.*

After practicing centering prayer for about twenty minutes, (using a kitchen timer to relieve you of the necessity of repeatedly checking your watch), gently open your eyes and return your attention to the room. You are likely to feel deeply relaxed and alert at the same time. Instead of jumping right up, stretch a bit and wait until your body is ready to return to your daily routine.

Though I practice Zen meditation most of the time, I find myself returning to centering prayer when I'm particularly stressed, as well as when I feel a longing for the devotional aspect of spirituality. It never fails to nourish my soul and make me whole.

The two forms of sitting meditation we have discussed are invaluable. But there are other ways to meditate that have their own special qualities. One of these is mindfulness meditation, and we'd like to acquaint you with two forms of this practice — walking meditation and lovingkindness meditation.

Walking Meditation

As we said earlier, Elizabeth and I traveled to the south of France shortly after our wedding for a two-week retreat with Thich Nhat Hanh, because we wanted to experience first-hand his form of mindfulness practice. His entire community at Plum Village is built on this practice, which he first wrote about in a book entitled *The Miracle of Mindfulness*. This book originated as a letter to some of his young followers, who had remained in Vietnam to minister to victims of the war still raging in that country after he had been forced into exile. They were experiencing what we would call "burn-out." Exhausted by their seemingly futile efforts to rebuild villages that had been bombed into oblivion as many as three or four times, they were on the verge of giving up. Nhat Hanh exhorted them to go back to their practice, to make a place for meditation in their lives, insisting that they could do so without abandoning the work to which they had committed themselves. The key, he said, was to be *mindful* in everything they did. By "mindfulness" he meant "keeping one's consciousness alive to the present reality."[2] This outlook, he maintained, is our link to eternity, "the miracle that can call back in a flash our dispersed mind and restore it to wholeness so that we can live each moment of life."[3]

During our initial orientation to Plum Village, Elizabeth and I were told that it was important that we take part in walking meditation, which occurs sometime every day. "If you have been to Plum Village and have not taken part in walking meditation," Sister Gina said, "you have not been to Plum Village." We were fortunate to have Thich Nhat Hanh himself as our leader the first time we participated. He patiently explained the practice before we set out as a group in a long column winding our way through the countryside. He began by saying that "practicing walking meditation is just practicing meditation while you walk." It has no goal, no fixed destination. The walking is not a means to get somewhere; it is an end in itself. If you walk mindfully, he said, each step should bring you back to the present moment. As you walk, don't imprint your anxiety or unhappiness on the ground, only peace and happiness. "How would you walk if you were in the kingdom of God?" he asked. "Walk that way now, and as you walk you will see this earth *become* the kingdom of God."

The problem is that we tend to fall into forgetfulness. We forget that we are truly alive this very moment. So we need a technique that will help us pay attention, and that technique is "conscious breathing" combined with counting. He suggested that we measure the length of our breaths by the number of steps we take with each inhalation and exhalation. As we watched, he slowly and deliberately demonstrated mindful walking. It was a beautiful sight, exuding peace and tranquility. He then turned to us and said, "I took three steps for each breath," as if he were discovering it for the first time. If your breath is even, you will find that you take the same number of steps with each breath, whether you are inhaling or exhaling. But if you are just beginning the practice, you will probably find that your exhalation is longer than your inhalation, in which case you will take more steps when you exhale than when you inhale, and that is all right. The important thing is to pay attention. Focus your attention on the contact between your foot and the ground. Think of yourself as planting peace with every step. The counting is useful, but not necessary. It binds your steps and your breathing into one, and thereby helps you to maintain awareness; but the object is to make happy, peaceful steps. If you can do that without counting, fine, but for most people counting helps.

Thomas Merton was once asked, "What is your practice?" He replied, "Walking in the woods." I sometimes think that I have been practicing walking meditation all of my life. Some times I practiced it on the golf course, other times on the college campus where I worked or during family outings to state parks near our home. But it took Thich Nhat Hanh to show me that what I was doing was a form of meditation. Walking meditation is a contemplative practice that almost anyone can do almost any time in life. I happen to think it is especially suitable to the Autumn Years, when we have more time at our disposal and may not be up to more strenuous forms of practice. It is particularly valuable in times of stress, when we may be too agitated to sit still for long periods of time. Walking and breathing mindfully at such times can help clear the mind and reestablish bodily equilibrium. It can be as much a path to inner peace as sitting meditation or centering prayer, and may be more accessible.

Lovingkindness Meditation

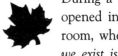 During a meditation retreat several years ago, a door opened in me that led to what seemed like a secret room, wherein this truth lived: *the substance in which we exist is Love.* I saw that underneath all the negative emotions, beyond all the traumatic memories, despite the tragedies in our lives, we are connected by love whether we

know it or not. Sharon Salzberg, a teacher of Vipassana (Insight Meditation), says it this way:

> Metta [lovingkindness] — the sense of love that is not bound to desire, that does not have to pretend that things are other than the way they are — overcomes the illusion of separateness, of not being part of a whole. Thereby metta overcomes all of the states that accompany this fundamental error of separateness — fear, alienation, loneliness, and despair — all the feelings of fragmentation. In place of these, the genuine realization of connectedness brings unification, confidence, and safety.[4]

The practice of lovingkindness meditation can help us to touch into that Love that underlies all other facets of our being. This form of contemplation begins with learning to love oneself, for until I can truly love myself, I cannot genuinely love any other person. It isn't a matter of developing something externally but of discovering the truth that Love is already my natural state! Here is the way to begin.

Sit quietly and relax with a few moments of deep breathing. Then recall a time when you did something for someone else that caused you to feel good about yourself. Mentally call up a picture of that time, remembering as many details as possible. Where were you? Look around in that place and see what's there. What did the person look like? Recall the facial expression, any body language. Relive the experience as clearly as you can. Now see if you can bring back the good feelings you had at the time.

Another way to come into this meditation is to think of some quality that you truly like about yourself, and allow yourself to bask in the grace of it. For me, it's the gift of imagination. I love this ability in myself and it has served me well in many ways. It's an unearned blessing that fills me with gratitude, and it's also an integral part of that ground of love that underlies all existence.

Spend some time this way, in appreciation of yourself. If critical voices try to destroy your good feelings, simply close the door to your secret room to shut out the negative thoughts and return to your meditation. Once you have some sense of loving yourself (even if it's meager at first), you are ready for the next phase. Begin to express the following desires for yourself, with as much sincerity as possible. Pause between statements to let them sink into your deep awareness.

> "May I be free from danger."
> "May I have mental happiness."
> "May I have physical happiness."
> "May I have ease of well-being."[5]

It's probably a good idea to memorize the statements because you will be using them again and again as you practice this form of meditation.

The next step in lovingkindness meditation is to express the same desires for someone you care about very much. Again, begin by calling up that person's image, her name, or just getting a feeling of her presence. Begin with someone who is still alive and who is not an object of sexual desire. Think of some quality about this person that you really like, and simply let yourself experience delight in that characteristic. Then repeat the lovingkindness phrases in her behalf, with true desire for her happiness, inserting her name ("May Mona be free from danger. May Mona . . . ")

The third phase of lovingkindness meditation is offered for the benefit of someone for whom your feelings are neutral. It might be a check-out person at the grocery store, or a casual acquaintance or neighbor, or any person who comes to mind for whom you have no particular feelings, either positive or negative. It's best to choose someone you see rather frequently so that you can visualize her clearly and also so that you can notice how your feelings about her change. Then, after calling up a mental picture of the person, offer the metta phrases in her behalf.

Now comes the hard part (although for many, the hardest person to feel lovingkindness toward is oneself!). Think of someone for whom you feel some negative emotion. It's best to begin with a person for whom your aversion is relatively mild. Again, it should be a living person with whom you come into contact. Later, you will gradually build up to offering lovingkindness meditation for that most difficult person in your life.

One person I've often chosen for the "mildly negative" part of the exercise is very critical in his words and actions toward me, as well as toward others I love. My original tendency was to avoid him as much as possible, but by doing so I was ignoring the fact that every person, at the deepest level, is made of the substance of love, and this is a fact I know to be true. So it became a challenge to me to see if I could find that ground of love in this man. In metta meditation, I focused on the fact that he is a true animal lover. He takes very good care of his dog and showers him with affection. As I practiced metta meditation for this person, I came to sense that he has a soft heart, even though it's covered over by the defensive need to criticize. Here's a quotation from the poet Rumi that has been very helpful to me in this: "Perhaps everything terrible is in its deepest being something that needs our love."[6] So if you find it difficult to express a desire for this person's well-being, Rumi's truth may help you, too.

Another aid in developing readiness for doing metta meditation for a difficult person is to think of her as a very young vulnerable child. For example, though my father could be very loving, he also had a terrible temper which caused me to fear him when I was a small child. Then one day I happened to come across a photograph of his family taken when my father was about five years old. He looked so very vulnerable, and even hurt, that I wanted to take him in my arms and love him back to wholeness! After that, I still feared his temper, but even my child mind had some understanding of his pain and the reason for his hurtful outbursts.

There is no time more appropriate for healing old grievances than during these waning years of our lives. We have lived long enough to know that everyone has faults and failings and to realize that holding grudges can eat up our hearts. The time has come for the healing of hearts. Lovingkindness meditation is a surprisingly effective tool to help us with this essential task.

Yoga

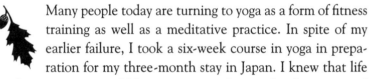 Many people today are turning to yoga as a form of fitness training as well as a meditative practice. In spite of my earlier failure, I took a six-week course in yoga in preparation for my three-month stay in Japan. I knew that life at the monastery would be strenuous and wanted to be in as good a shape as possible. My body, which was not very flexible to begin with, had developed a number of bad habits over the years and needed some retraining. I did not look to yoga for a contemplative practice (sitting meditation was my practice of choice), but to my surprise I found that it was very contemplative, that the stretching exercises I did every morning could bring me to a state of deep peace and tranquility. Breathing helped me to get into the various yoga postures, while the postures themselves represented a still point not unlike what I found in sitting meditation. These exercises accomplished their main purpose, which was to prepare me for life in the monastery. But they also afforded a healthy balance to the many hours of sitting I was required to do while I was

there and provided an alternative form of meditative practice that I came to value for its own sake. Scarcely a day went by when I did not complete my yoga routine, and feel better for it.

When I returned to the United States, I continued to do these exercises, though not as faithfully. When Elizabeth and I got together, we decided to incorporate a gentle form of yoga into our daily schedule. We do not see it as taking the place of sitting meditation or centering prayer, but rather as a complement. The body, in our view, is not separate from the mind. By gently stretching our limbs, breathing into each movement, often to the accompaniment of music, we feel that we are doing for the body what meditation does for the mind. There are more ambitious forms of yoga that you might want to consider, but the gentle form that we practice seems particularly well suited to our time in life.

We took a yoga class soon after we moved to Colorado. The instructor, a young woman named Teryl, introduced us to a number of yoga postures, many of which we continue to use, but what we have found most helpful is a sequence of stretching movements that she calls "standing warm-ups for yoga." The sequence goes like this:

- Feet and ankles: wiggle toes; circle ankles; rock on toes and heels.

- Knees: circle first one way and then the other (but not if you have knee problems).

- Pelvis: hands on hips, circle both ways.

- Hands: wiggle fingers; circle wrists; form and release fists.

- Shoulders: Hands on shoulders, circle elbows both ways; hands to side, circle shoulders both ways.

- Reach and stretch arms in all directions: up, forward, side, back.

- Clasp hands behind back and twist both ways.
- Let head drop toward each shoulder; look over each shoulder, keeping body forward; raise and lower chin.
- Slide left arm down leg, raising right elbow toward ceiling. Reverse.
- Arch left arm over head and bend to left. Reverse.
- Swing arms back and forth.
- Reach straight up and then lean to each side without bending forward.
- Bend forward at waist and let arms fall in front (creating a rag doll effect).

The whole sequence can be completed in about ten minutes. It is, as the name suggests, a good warm-up for other yoga exercises, but it is an excellent relaxing exercise in its own right. In the workshops we lead, we use it to introduce centering prayer and in retreats we attend we often use it to help us relax between periods of sitting. You too might want to find a way of incorporating physical movement into your meditative practice.

Lectio Divina

In his introduction to contemplative prayer, Thomas Keating speaks of a form of spiritual practice, employed by monastics and laity alike in the early centuries of the Christian church, called *lectio divina* or "sacred reading." It involves close, personal reading of scripture, or more precisely attentive "listening to scripture," with the objective of cultivating ever deeper levels of inward attention to the word of God. Close reading of a text is followed by reflection on its meaning, which in turn leads to affective prayer or opening one's heart to God, and finally to contemplative prayer or "resting in the presence of God." Contemplation is thus seen as a normal outcome of listening to the word of God. In time, however, these different phases were compartmentalized and separated until the contemplative aspect was almost entirely lost. Yet in Keating's view they belong together.[7] Sacred reading of a text can help prepare one for contemplative prayer, while contemplative prayer can deepen one's understanding of the text.

During my term as a resident scholar at the Institute for Ecumenical and Cultural Research, I received some training in *lectio divina* from one of the sisters at a nearby Catholic women's college. I can personally attest that this meditative practice is an excellent complement to sitting meditation or centering prayer. While either of the latter two practices can take you to a place of deep inward silence, they can also help prepare you for hearing the word of God in scripture. I especially liked sacred reading of the psalms — usually just a single passage from one of the psalms — following a half-hour of sitting meditation. I would first read the passage slowly, noticing particular words or phrases that attracted my attention. I would repeat those words several times so that they could become a part of me, pondering their meaning and listening for whatever message they might have for my life. Once I felt the words had touched my heart, I would consciously place myself at the disposal of God's will for me. Finally, I would return to the silence of my earlier meditation, resting in the realization that God is present in me and in all things.

Elizabeth not only used this practice at an earlier time in her life, she wrote about it in a lovely book entitled *Where Soul and Spirit Meet.*[8] This book is a guide to praying with the Bible and a complement to her earlier book about meditation. She has found that for most Christians, meditative reflection on scripture is a valuable addition to contemplative prayer as a way of deepening one's relationship with God.

Koan Study

 One of the most evocative meditative practices available is koan study, which comes out of the Zen tradition. A koan is an enigmatic statement or story or dialogue that is designed to throw off the logical, linear, conceptual part of the mind so that deeper insights from the more creative part of the mind can come forth. Koan work accesses the unconscious mind, for which I have a most profound respect. Through this mental medium have come the greatest works of art, poetry, and music, as well as the most innovative ideas in all fields of endeavor. The unconscious mind is accessed in dreams, active imagination, and spontaneous images, as well as through koans. We've all had the experience of trying to remember a name without success and then later, when our minds are otherwise occupied, having the name suddenly present itself. Koan work is a bit like that. You may try very hard to "figure out" an answer, or get the point of a koan without success, but if you sit with it in meditation, allowing it to float freely and easily in your mind, a bright and surprising insight may arise. This kind of sudden realization may also appear while you're walking to the post office, or putting in a washing, or taking care of a grandchild.

Koan study is one of my favorite meditative practices, but I won't write about it in any detail here because of the fact that it requires interaction with a teacher knowledgeable in the practice. Unless you have found a Zen teacher who works with koans, it's almost impossible to do this practice. I know this from experience. Before I met my present teacher, Joan Sutherland, I had tried several times to work with koans and reaped nothing but frustration. Now that I have a teacher, I've found that shining new vistas keep opening as I work with the koans she gives me.

Just to whet your appetite for finding a teacher to work with on koans, I'd like to quote a passage from a recently published pamphlet by John Tarrant.

Working with a koan can make the world more transparent and alive and at the same time shift your consciousness in small and large ways. It's a work of art as well as a spiritual method and intended to be useful in your life and contribute to your happiness.[9]

If you'd like to try a koan, here is a question you could hold as you meditate, and as you go about your daily routine: "Who hears?" This question is especially appropriate to let float within you during music meditation.

Music Meditation

Another meditative practice that Robert and I have found to be quite wonderful is music meditation. You don't need to be a musician; you don't even have to know anything about music to borrow its wings. All you need is a tape or CD player and some inspiring music. Headphones enhance the experience but are not a necessity. We enjoy classical music, particularly the uplifting strains of such composers as Bach, Beethoven, and Mozart, but you should choose the type of music you most enjoy, with this caveat: it's best to select something that is not too stimulating and is without vocalization. Try to arrange it so that the music will play continuously for at least thirty minutes.

Background music is one thing, but music meditation another. We prefer to practice music meditation at night, with only a night light or candle for illumination, so we won't be distracted by visual stimuli. Usually, we kick back in our recliners to listen, but the practice can be done just as well sitting in a chair or lying down. Yes, sometimes we fall asleep but that's okay. Our unconscious minds are still wide awake and absorbing the experience! Just let go of any cares or concerns of the day and let the music carry you. Listen with your heart, not your ears. Just climb onto the music and ride with it. Let yourself merge into the timeless, spaceless vastness of the Absolute. You'll find that, at some point, there is no stereo player, no room, no you. There is only the music. When the last chords fade, in the silence of that moment, offer yourself into the eternal stillness. Remain in this Presence as long as you like and then gradually return to the room, stretch a bit, and when you're ready, turn on the lights and return to your evening routine.

May you know yourself to be a singing note in the one eternal song.

CHAPTER FIVE

Supporting Your Practice

It takes courage to sit well. We have to be willing to do something that is not easy. If we do it with patience and perseverance, with the guidance of a good teacher, then gradually our life settles down, becomes more balanced. CHARLOTTE JOKO BECK

Before my first trip to Japan, I decided that I ought to learn to speak some Japanese — nothing too ambitious, just a few commonly used expressions that could help me to get around in a country where not everyone speaks English. The language turned out to be far more daunting than I expected. Some of the sounds used in speaking Japanese are not present in English, while written Japanese is totally different from written English. It was a challenge just to retain these words long enough to say them back to the teacher, much less use them correctly in a conversation. But then Eiko, my Japanese language teacher, said something that I found particularly valuable. Encouraging me to keep up my practice, no matter how much (or how little) progress I seemed to be making, she reminded me of the expression "practice makes perfect." When it comes to language study, she observed, it would be more accurate to say "practice makes permanent."

That is also true of meditation practice. We can, as in so many other pursuits, get caught up in trying to do it "just right." Listening to Harada Roshi, my Zen teacher in Japan, demonstrate the proper way to breathe, I despaired of ever being able to breathe

like that. As hard as I tried, I could not make my breath sound like his. It was a standard of perfection I could never reach. But why should I? Maybe that was not the point of my practice. Recalling my language teacher's admonition, I have decided it is enough just to practice. The more I practice the more habitual the practice becomes. It is not yet "second nature" for me to attend to my breath, but I'm getting there. When stressful situations come up, I'm much more likely to notice my breath and consciously slow down. I now have a way of restoring equilibrium and achieving a measure of inward tranquility that I did not previously have. We call meditation a "practice" because it is something we *do,* as in the Greek root *praxis*; but it is also something we do repeatedly in order that it might in time become an enduring part of who we are.

One reason that people go to live in a monastery is so that they can pursue their contemplative practice in a supportive environment. Since most of us do not have the inclination (or the freedom) to live in a monastery, we have to look for other ways to support our practice. Elizabeth and I will talk about some of those ways, including the value of having a teacher, a sacred space, and a community of practitioners.

Making Your Practice Regular

 Meditation can bring order into everyday life, but only if *we* first order our day to include a time for it. In physics there's a phenomenon called the Meissner effect. When certain metals and alloys are placed in magnetic fields and then cooled to a sufficiently low temperature, an interesting thing happens. The electrons, which had been in a state of disordered random motion, enter into an ordered state.

Like those electrons in their state of random motion, most of us are so strongly influenced by forces outside of ourselves that our energies are constantly scattered. Because of this, we use up tremendous amounts of energy to accomplish very little. Yet when we temporarily withdraw our energies from the external world through meditation, we "cool down" that inner agitation and our minds become serene, uncluttered, orderly. If we do this regularly, over a period of time that "cooled out" state will carry over into our daily lives, providing us with a valuable degree of immunity from disrupting external influences. When one meditates regularly there is, in time, a *meditation mood* that pervades the consciousness at all times so that when the mind is not occupied with matters of the day, the attention naturally turns within to contemplation.

Here are some very specific things you can do to stimulate that meditative mood and the ordered life that results from regularity of practice:

Check your priorities. The first and most obvious thing to do is to rearrange your priorities so that meditation is the one thing in the day that you absolutely will not let yourself skip, no matter what else comes up. This is a bit off-putting at first. On a packed-full day, I've often thought, "I just don't have time to meditate today." But I've learned that those are exactly the days I most need it!

When I was a young married woman with children and a new lawn to take care of, I had trouble dividing my time between the housework and the yard work, but I soon learned that, if I got my inside work done first, I could do the outside work with a clearer mind. Meditation is the "inside work" that clears our mind and orders the events of our day.

Make a Contemplation Covenant. It may seem rather silly, but it's supportive to write out your vow to spend time in meditation each day. If you think you don't have time to schedule in meditation, I'd suggest you make a list of all the daily demands on your time. Then imagine you're a hundred years old and looking back on your life. From that perspective, which things are most important? Which have lasting value?

If possible, it's good to sit twice a day, but it's better to sit once than not at all. In the beginning, I'd suggest starting with a single sitting each day until you are able to be faithful to that. Then you may choose to add a second sitting. We've found that sitting in the early morning before breakfast is a delightful way to start the day. It's also a good time for sitting because the mind is not yet cluttered with the events of the day. It just seems to help us to start the morning in a state of equanimity, and it often happens that the rest of the day then unfolds in a more orderly and less stressful way. However, early morning sitting doesn't work well for me if I've lost sleep the night before, or if I wake with a headache. Some folks need a cup of coffee to begin the day, and it's fine to have that first. It's just best not to sit right after a meal because the digestive process interferes with mental clarity.

Evening sitting needs to be timed to your body's natural rhythm. It's best to plan your meditation time when you're not likely to be overly tired. At one time Robert and I were sitting each evening just before bed, and I often found myself hardly able to keep my eyes open, let alone to focus my mind. It was a waste of time. Sitting earlier in the evening is much better for me.

Meditation practice is not like going out for dinner on special occasions, but more like the evening supper that husband and wife share each day — nothing special, just daily nourishment. Anything less than daily sitting is likely to result in spiritual malnutrition.

Establish a regular place for meditation. Having a special place for meditation, a sacred space, helps you to settle in more easily by creating a mental set and an air of expectancy, so that when you enter that special room and sit in that same chair, your mind automatically begins to calm down and tune in. It doesn't have to be a room set aside *only* for that purpose, although if you have a spare room, that's great. Robert and I have found it increases our sense of sacredness to have a small altar, with a meaningful symbol or two, a candle, perhaps some incense and occasionally flowers in the room. If the room is used for other purposes, these items can be stored when not in use.

Your sacred space should be a place where you can count on being alone (or with a sitting companion), without being interrupted. I know this is difficult for many people but if you really want to do it, you'll find a way. When I lived in Nebraska, I had a friend who lived in a small apartment with her husband and two little children. She meditated in her parked car. It is said that the mother of John and Charles Wesley, who couldn't find a corner in her house to be alone, would sit in a kitchen chair and put her large apron over her head, which said to her family: "Please do not disturb. I am at prayer." I'm sure this was a more eloquent statement to her children about the importance of God in her daily life than all the preaching in the world!

Minimize distractions. Take the phone off the hook or turn off the ringer. If you're home alone, put a note on the outside door. It can be very simple: "Please do not disturb between 11:00 and 11:30 a.m. Thank you." If you simply cannot find a quiet place to meditate, buy a pair of earplugs. The wax-impregnated kind is the most effective.

Shorten instead of skipping. On those days in which you honestly cannot possibly take out twenty or twenty-five minutes for quiet time, meditate for five minutes, or whatever you can spare. It's better than skipping because it maintains your vow and keeps the regularity going.

Practice even if nothing is happening. There are times when nothing seems to be happening during the meditation period, or when the mind insists on wandering throughout. When that happens, negative thoughts arise, such as "I'm just wasting my time and getting nowhere. What's the use of this, anyway? Is it really doing anything good?" Let me assure you that even during those times, something important *is* happening. Even though the conscious mind won't behave, things are happening within. The results of meditation are cumulative. You will know this after you've established a regular practice and kept at it long enough to see the long-term effects.

Having said all this, I need to be honest and tell you that Robert and I are not always faithful to our meditation commitment. When one of us isn't feeling well, or when we're unusually busy, or tired, we are quite capable of talking ourselves out of it. Unfortunately, missing once makes it easier to miss again — and again. If this happens to you (and it probably will), don't beat up on yourself. Simply begin again. Renew your commitment to daily meditation, and let go of any guilt feelings, just as you have learned to let go of wandering thoughts during meditation. It is never too late for a new beginning, and the rewards are priceless.

The Value of Having a Teacher

There is a saying, "when the student is ready the teacher appears." Yet I can remember a time when I wanted to take up the practice of meditation but lacked a teacher. My efforts to practice on my own, like Elizabeth's efforts to do koan study on her own, came to naught. But maybe I was not ready. I didn't make much effort to find a teacher during the time that I first began experimenting with meditation. Many years later, returning from China, where I had the privilege of visiting a Zen temple and seeing the place where monks had been meditating for over a thousand years, I was inspired to find a teacher — and lo, the teacher appeared.

Ben Wren admitted me to his advanced workshop even though I had not taken the introductory workshop. He showed me the fundamentals of sitting, and more importantly he modeled them.

In that five-day workshop we did more than just sit. He introduced us to the ancient art of calligraphy, showing us how to make Chinese characters in black ink on newsprint. One afternoon was devoted to *ikebana*, traditional Japanese flower arranging, with each of us gathering flowers from the nearby countryside and arranging them in vases according to the prescribed forms. Ben also taught us a form of *tai chi*, the ancient Chinese practice of moving meditation, gracefully leading us through the various movements to the strains of Pachelbel's Canon. In the evening he celebrated the Eucharist with us, incorporating these same movements into the Christian liturgy. What I learned from him was not just the basics of sitting meditation, but a whole assortment of ways to express the contemplative spirit. I was inspired to take the contemplative path! I might have done so anyway, but his example definitely had an influence.

Elizabeth and I have sought out teachers who could model for us different forms of meditative practice. We went to Plum Village in order learn more about mindfulness practice from Thich Nhat Hanh and to Japan to deepen our practice of sitting meditation with my former teacher Harada Roshi. More recently we have established an ongoing relationship with two teachers in California, Joan Sutherland and David Weinstein, both of whom have had extensive training in traditional Zen practices but are committed to giving creative expression to these practices in forms consistent with contemporary American culture. They take turns coming to Colorado several times a year to lead retreats, in which they give public talks and meet privately with their students for koan study. They also conduct phone interviews, in which they work with us on koans. Some Zen practitioners would think that there is a basic inconsistency in this combination of the contemporary and the traditional, but we feel that we have the best of both worlds.

My point is that everyone must find his own way. Do not assume that every teacher is going to present Zen meditation (or

Christian contemplative practice) in the same way. It is all right to shop around, attend workshops, hear talks by various teachers, perhaps visit several different meditation groups before deciding which teacher or which form of practice is best for you. Even then you need not assume that your decision is for all time. (We have a stone, given to us by a friend, on which is carved the saying, "Nothing is carved in stone.") Since contemplative practice at its best is a developing process, a particular teacher may be right for you at one time and another teacher at a later time.

You have no doubt heard of spiritual teachers in various traditions who were very authoritarian and who required absolute devotion from their students. That has not been our experience. We have gravitated to teachers who spoke with authority based on their personal experience, but were not authoritarian. They were like spiritual friends whom we could trust to guide us along the path, pick us up when we fell down, and give us a shove when we needed it.

Though there are individuals who can maintain a good contemplative practice without a teacher, we have found it extremely valuable to have a wise person with years of experience with whom to discuss the things that come up in meditation, a person to whom we can bring questions, doubts, and frustrations. A good teacher can also provide encouragement and impart wisdom that is available in no other way. So I'd encourage you to seek out a teacher with whom you feel an affinity. But if there is none available in your area, there are other ways to support your practice.

Other Teaching Resources

When I first began teaching about Eastern religions in the early 1960s, there were very few books dealing with the *practices* of these religions. There were some excellent historical and theoretical works on Buddhism, Hinduism and Taoism, the three great meditative traditions of the East, but nothing that would tell a person how to meditate. The same was true of the Christian contemplative tradition. Even the writings of Thomas Merton, which did so much to kindle a general interest in contemplative practice among Christians, offered very little in the way of practical advice. But that has all changed. Beginning in the late 1960s, books began to appear in ever increasing numbers specifically designed to introduce people to the practice of meditation. So today there are many excellent books of this sort to choose from.

My three favorites are Shunryu Suzuki's book *Zen Mind, Beginner's Mind*, a beautifully written introduction to traditional sitting meditation; Thich Nhat Hanh's *Miracle of Mindfulness*, originally intended as a manual for young social activists but accessible to anyone interested in taking up the practice of mindfulness meditation; and for Christians, Thomas Keating's *Open Mind, Open Heart*, an excellent introduction to centering prayer. Suzuki is no longer living, but the other two are still active teachers who give retreats, workshops and lectures that you might want to attend. There are also tapes of their talks that are readily available.

Elizabeth has purchased several series of tapes over the years and found them quite valuable in strengthening her practice. One of her favorites is a correspondence course on *Insight Meditation* taught by Sharon Salzberg and Joseph Goldstein. Based on the curriculum developed at the Insight Meditation Society's retreat center in Barre, Massachusetts, it is designed to help you develop and sustain a daily meditation practice. But not all of the books you'll want to read or tapes you'll want to listen to are of this "how-to" variety. Some are primarily inspirational or consist mainly of reflections on the practice of meditation intended to deepen your understanding of and appreciation for the contemplative path. Of course, reading about meditation is of little value unless you choose a form and practice it regularly.

Practicing Together

Find a sitting partner. In addition to the suggestions we've offered for making one's practice regular — finding a good teacher and using books, tapes and workshops as supports — there is one more extremely valuable and heartening aid to the practice of meditation. It is having someone with whom to practice.

After I had learned the basics of Zen meditation, I thought I could just practice it at home. After all, I was living alone at the time and had few interruptions. However, I found this to be extremely difficult. There was a certain inertia that set in after a few weeks, and I found it hard to get myself to actually begin a sit. If I got past that hindrance, I was surprised to find myself wanting to get up before the period was over. I remember one night in particular; I had been sitting for about ten minutes when I caught myself thinking, *I'm hungry. I guess I'll go get a banana!* That was when I started going to Kearney Zendo every evening and sitting with Yozan and whoever happened to be there. It was a tremendous help to me! Just knowing that someone was expecting me overcame the inertia, and I began to look forward to the sittings. I often sat there in the mornings also, much to the benefit of my practice.

Then, after Robert and I were married, we found that sitting together provided a bonding beyond any we'd known before, and it kept us regular in our practice. At those times when I might have skipped, all Robert had to say was, "Well, it's time for us to sit," and the inertia disappeared. I think it worked both ways. We helped to keep each other faithful.

Unless you're an unusually self-disciplined person, you might find sitting alone difficult, too. Perhaps there is someone among your friends or family members who would be interested in learning to meditate, who might become your sitting partner. Believe

me, it will bring you into a much closer and more rewarding relationship. I urge you to take the risk of asking. Or, if you belong
to a meditation or centering prayer group, you might find someone in the group who also needs the support of a regular sitting
partner.

Find a spiritual community. One morning, a few months after
Robert and I were married, I woke with an insistent longing I
didn't understand. I knew it wasn't dissatisfaction with our marriage. I had never in my life felt so happy and fulfilled. What could
possibly be missing? Rather than to try to figure it out, I began
to sit with the question. A few days later Robert said something
about "community," and it went straight into my heart where the
ache was.

When we were first married, we were so busy setting up a
household that all we wanted was to be with each other. We kept
talking about finding a church and we visited a few, but we didn't
feel a real need to belong. Since we meditated together, we felt we
were already a community of two. But could it be that wholeness
in a relationship calls for a third dimension — the dimension of
reaching out together?

It was then that we began an active search for a spiritual community. We checked the church listings in the yellow pages and
found a Vipassana meditation group, so we attended several of
their meetings and a retreat. Then someone mentioned that there
was also a Zen group in Colorado Springs and gave us a name to
call. Sarah Bender was very welcoming and invited us to attend
the Monday evening sitting of Springs Mountain Sangha, a lay
group with California teachers who led retreats and stayed in
touch with their students by telephone. The members were warm
and friendly, and though the liturgy was somewhat different from
what we were used to, we found it to our liking. We had found
our home. Now we are an active part of the group, sitting with

them on Monday evenings and Saturday mornings, as well as attending and sometimes hosting half-day or whole-day sits, and of course participating in retreats when our teachers are here. Like the foundation for our home, Springs Mountain Sangha provides solid grounding for our meditation practice.

To find a meditation group or a church where centering prayer is practiced, check the yellow pages, search the web, and ask around. If you already belong to a church that has no contemplative dimension, consider starting a group. You might invite a speaker or speakers to give a workshop on centering prayer or other contemplative practices as a starter for the group. I think you'll find that being part of a centering prayer group or a community of meditators will deepen and broaden your prayer life and help you to discover the great truth that we are all vital organs in one divine body, "individually members one of another."[1]

The Paradox of Solitude

Before I took up the practice of meditation, I wondered why such a solitary practice was so often carried on within a community. Thomas Merton grappled with this paradox most of his adult life. He needed the structure of a strict monastic community in order to realize the profound inner freedom that contemplative practice made possible. Yet he also rebelled against it, seeking ever more solitude for himself until finally he was granted permission to live as a hermit on the outskirts of the monastery. Even then he was not content, toying with the idea of establishing his own community while maintaining a far-flung correspondence with some of the leading intellectuals of the day. Solitude, it seems, is not complete without community, while community requires solitude to give it inner depth.

In the "community of practice" to which Elizabeth and I belong, we also confront this paradox. Every one of us has a great

many demands on his time and difficult life situations to deal
with — and we know how hard it can be to keep up the practice of meditation without the support of others. So we value
this community and work hard to maintain it. Yet like all human
communities it has its conflicts; misunderstandings occur, egos
are bruised, and feelings get hurt. I'm sure we have all thought at
one time or another: "I don't need this. I can do just as well by
myself." But then sitting in meditation, we come to realize that
we are not separate after all and the pain we attribute to others
has its origin in ourselves. So our practice deepens our ties to the
community, even as the community supports our practice.

CHAPTER SIX

Relationship as Practice

The act of conscious attending to another person — when one once discovers the taste of it and its significance — can become the center of gravity of the work of love.

JACOB NEEDLEMAN

The dream that launched me on my spiritual journey (the one that came in the middle of a meditation retreat) prompted some serious self-examination on my part. I had begun the practice of meditation a year earlier, and while my practice was irregular I could see that it was having an effect — just not the effect I'd expected. Instead of greater peace of mind, I was feeling more dissatisfied with myself and more uncertain of my future. I had professional accomplishments to my credit and no great unfulfilled career aspirations, so that was not the problem. Something more basic was lacking. I concluded that perhaps I was neglecting my spiritual life. It was then that I began to think about retirement as a time to develop this aspect of myself, but I didn't know how to get started.

So I signed up for a directed retreat with Sister Maureen, a retired nun serving part-time on the staff of St. Mary of the Pines, a nearby retirement community for the School Sisters of Notre Dame that also served as a retreat center. We had met on an earlier occasion, and she had impressed me as a very discerning person. I told her about my interest in preparing for retirement, and she encouraged me to imagine "a future without parameters."

Circumstance will impose constraints, she acknowledged, but first we must let our imagination reach out to what we most want. What would you do, she asked, if you were to retire tomorrow? And what can you do now to prepare for that day whenever it comes? She thought that I had some unique gifts that I could put to use in my retirement, and we spoke of some of these. But then she said something that took me completely by surprise: "You are a contemplative."

I had never thought of myself as a contemplative. I had lived a very active life, in which I defined myself largely through my accomplishments. Could it be there was a contemplative dimension present without my realizing it? I had only recently taken up meditation as a form of contemplative practice, but perhaps that was not the only way to be a contemplative. Sister Maureen wanted me to follow a formal meditative practice, such as centering prayer, since it could provide what she called a "platform for discernment," but she could see that there was already a contemplative dimension to my life. She could see it in my work and my personal relationships, especially my relationships with my children. By pursuing a formal practice, she thought I could deepen this aspect of my life.

In the ensuing years, I have found that to be the case. The practice of meditation has made me aware that *everything I do can have a contemplative dimension.* Walking to the post office, weeding the garden, washing the dishes: no activity is so ordinary that it cannot be a form of contemplative practice. Yet of all the places in my life where I see this practice at work, none has been more deeply affected than my relationship with Elizabeth. Attending to one another, supporting one another in our spiritual journeys, has become for us a primary form of contemplative practice. This development has in turn provided an opening for *intimacy* such as neither of us supposed possible.

Intimacy in Relationships

 "How can contemplation foster intimacy?" my friend asked as we sat in a quiet little coffee shop over tea. "I've always thought of meditation as an isolating, even self-centered practice." Though her comment took me aback, I think it's only fair to say that meditation *can become* that. If one takes up the practice as a way of escaping from the world and life's problems and never grows beyond that, she may get lost in egoistic concerns and become something of a recluse. However, when rightly practiced, meditation brings true self-awareness, a state of being that leads beyond ego. As Zen Master Dogen has written, "To study Zen is to study the self. To study the self is to forget the self. To forget the self is to be enlightened by all things."[1] This realization of the Greater Self, not isolation, is the more valid result of regular contemplative practice.

So why is it so difficult for most people to achieve genuine intimacy? A. H. Almaas offers this answer: it is impossible for the *ego* to make true contact with another person.[2] We are conditioned beings, with many defenses that wall us in, creating invisible barriers that tend to discourage those who try to get to know us better. But I've discovered that meditation can be a solvent that melts away some of my old walls and defenses, helping me to *let others in,* so that I can relate much more authentically and intimately.

Intimacy occurs when two people reach over the tops of their own invisible walls of self-protection and clasp hands. Then gradually, brick by brick, they can risk letting the other person see more and more of who they really are. Each time we share a dream, admit a fear, or reveal a memory, we remove a brick of the wall. As we share — and keep — confidences, our trust builds and we gain courage to reveal more of ourselves. Though the wall will never be completely eliminated (and probably shouldn't be), intimacy risks exposure for the sake of touching on a deeper level. It can be frightening, but how great are the rewards! To feel that you are truly known by another human being is deeply freeing. The bridge to intimacy is not made of self-assurance but of the ability to be vulnerable. When both people practice meditation, they invariably become more open and therefore vulnerable. They can then welcome each other's openness, providing common ground for inner growth.

Another way in which ego (our conditioned self-image) prevents intimacy is that we often tend to relate to others, not as the unique beings they are, but as we related to our parents and others who influenced us early in life. This transference makes us unable to see each other clearly. For example, when I unconsciously associate Robert with old memories of my father, I may interpret things he says as being critical, even though he didn't intend them to be. Or I may think he's treating me like a child when he's simply showing concern for my welfare. As part of our practice, we can help each other to become aware of such transferences.

Fear of being alone can also be a strong barrier to intimacy. Many of us, whether consciously or unconsciously, tend to fill up our time in ways that prevent us from coming to know our true selves. I think it's one of "Murphy's laws" that busyness will expand to fill the time available. However, if one can just get past the fear of having to face oneself, she may discover that intentionally spending some time alone can be one of life's most rewarding experiences, and the Autumn Years can provide an ideal opening for us to *make* time to be present with the great vastness to which we belong. In contemplative solitude it is possible to touch into that part of ourselves that is most authentic, most true, most connected to the divine nature. And surprise! This is exactly the part that is also most connected with all beings! It is the place at which we discover what Thich Nhat Hanh calls *interbeing.* We come to know that we are already, and always have been, one with all living beings. For such awareness to happen, one must be in touch with what Almaas calls the *Essential Self*.[3] Though I prefer to use the terms, the *Light within* or *Divine Nature*, contemplative practice is the best vehicle I know for touching into that unitive reality, from whose ground we may reach out to others with love, acceptance, and authenticity.

Intimacy is not clinging or possessive. Rather, it is two people standing together, touching emotionally and spiritually, sometimes physically if appropriate, and letting go, free to move together or separately, each knowing that the other person will be there for them when they need a listening ear, a gentle prod, or someone to say, "Here, let me carry that heavy load for a little while."

I love to watch the paired figure skating performances during the winter Olympics because they create for me an ideal picture of an intimate relationship. The skaters sometimes move along side by side; sometimes they come together and move in delightful unison; then they move apart, soloing with grace and controlled freedom, coming together again when it's right. The beauty of the ice dance includes movements in which one skater lifts or carries the other, which means one skater must be willing to be lifted or carried by the other. All of this is part of what it means to be intimate. But like the ice dance, it requires regularly practicing together. In fact, the dance itself can become the practice.

Robert and I are learning this rewarding practice of true intimacy during our later years, after having failed to find the kind of closeness we longed for in our previous marriages — though we certainly do not feel this practice is limited to married couples. We'd like to share with you some of the practical ways in which *relationship as practice* is happening in our marriage as well as in some of our other close relationships.

Resolving Differences

Learning to resolve our differences in a mature way is a practice by which we can help each other to grow in unity of soul and spirit. For example, my friend Jan and I decided, from the beginning of our friendship, to talk about our issues as they came up rather than to let them smolder inside, creating resentment. This is as important in friendship as it is in marriage.

Because we talk frankly and honestly about the relationships in our lives (including our own friendship) and many other personal things, we often find that, after we've had lunch together, there's something that feels unfinished or uncomfortable. When that happens, we call each other and say, "I've got to process a twinge." Sometimes it's just a little thing we wish we hadn't said, or something that didn't come out the way we meant it, or a comment the other person made that stung a little. I think it's this practice of "processing our twinges" that makes it possible for us to be completely open with each other, not having to weigh our words or hide behind defenses. It's the sort of thing that helps people to stay close in any relationship.

Family relationships can also be enriched by the authenticity that arises when we can get out from behind our defenses. My daughter Karen used to have a pet hedgehog who often ran behind her sofa and then fanned out his quills, so he was stuck in his own defense mechanism and couldn't get out until he calmed down and relaxed those protective quills. One day, Karen and I were having an argument and both of us were getting defensive. This must have upset Hedgie, who did his usual hiding trick. Suddenly, we both burst out laughing, realizing we were doing exactly the same thing! We were hiding behind our defenses and "spreading out our quills." In that state, there was no way we could get out of our self-imposed captivity long enough to resolve our differences.

Being able to laugh at ourselves helped us to break through our impasse and come to agreement.

In the fourteen years that I've been practicing Zen meditation, I've found that, though I still occasionally have defensive reactions, such misunderstandings are less likely to occur, and when they do they're more easily cleared up. Again, it's that *solvent* capacity of meditation that makes the difference. One begins to notice, while sitting in the silence, that all kinds of emotions arise — anger, pride, fear, joy, resentment, hope, self-aggrandizement and self-criticism, jealousy, envy, admiration, worry, desire and aversion, almost every known emotion shows its face at some time. But there's another thing that one begins to observe: emotions are impermanent. They arise and they fall away. For example, one evening when I was sitting with Yozan, I realized I had some feelings of anger at my son John (then a teenager) about his recent behavior. So I just kept breathing into my anger, and by the end of the evening (consisting of two forty-minute sittings separated by walking meditation) I had "breathed into" my anger and released it so many times, I couldn't for the life of me remember what I was upset with John about! Of course, once I was home, it came back to me but I could now discuss it with him calmly and without undue anger.

On another occasion, here in Colorado during one of our four-period Saturday sits, a negative emotion arose, one that had troubled me off and on all my life. Almost as soon as it did, I had the tremendously freeing realization that *I don't need that emotion anymore!* This was followed by, *Maybe I never did!* And I wondered, *When did that change for me?* Clearly, it had happened so gradually I hadn't been aware of the inner movement. The emotion still arises on occasion but when it does, I find it so much easier to release. It doesn't have a chance to get in the driver's seat and take over my attitude. It is not unusual, among meditators who have been practicing for some time, to find old emotional patterns dissolving.

Robert and I have found that, when one of us experiences hurt or angry feelings in reaction to something the other has said or done, it's often best to wait a while before talking about it, to sit with it in meditation, allowing the solvent to break up the ·intensity of the feelings. Then (a few hours later or the next day) we can sit down and talk about it and the other person can listen with an open heart. It helps, sometimes, to mirror back to the person who is feeling emotional pain, what you're hearing. For example, if Robert says, "Why won't you let me help get ready for company?" I might respond with, "It sounds as if you're feeling left out." He might respond with, "That's not quite it. It feels as though you're taking over and I'm just standing around. It makes me feel unnecessary." If we keep listening, mirroring, and then correcting our understanding about what the other feels, eventually empathy enters, bearing its gift of understanding. The important thing is for the person with a grievance to feel truly heard. You can mirror back to your friend or spouse or partner what you think she's feeling even if you disagree with her about the issue in question. Once she's able to say, "Yes, you really heard me. That's the way I feel," then it's your turn to express your feelings and the process is reversed. When each has truly touched into the other's feelings, the need to be "right" has dissolved. I once heard a talk by a Zen master who assured his listeners that there is one fail-proof way to keep a relationship healthy. He put it in just six words:

"Stop making the other person wrong."[4]

Meditation disposes us to listen deeply so we can hear the pain beneath angry words, and this dissolves our need to prove ourselves right. Then we're ready to talk about how to resolve the situation. This is a practice of *interbeing* by which we come to realize the universal nature of our basic humanity.

Facing Our Shadow

"Sometimes you treat me like a child!" Elizabeth's words came unexpectedly and went straight to my heart. We were on our way to an appointment, and I asked her if she had remembered to bring some papers we needed. What was so wrong with that? Of course, I didn't think she was a child; I saw her as an extremely intelligent, exceptionally competent person. But she was telling me that I didn't always treat her that way, and that was hard to hear. Her words cut into my image of myself and exposed a contradiction between what I thought and what I did. I thought I respected her independence and valued our relationship as equals, yet, as her words revealed, I could, on occasion, assume the role of a parent and treat her like a child.

Later that day we talked about what had happened, and she acknowledged some projection on her part. It was one of those situations in which she responded to me as if I were her father, when clearly I am not. But that did not take away from the fact that I was treating her as if she were not a fully responsible adult. Truth be told, I wanted to be in control. In my inflated image of myself, I was the responsible one: everything depended on me. I could not allow her to be a person in her own right.

This is my *shadow* side, that part of me I don't want to acknowledge, even to myself. It comes out in my relationship with Elizabeth because we are intimately related. I am more vulnerable in relation to her than anyone else, and so feel a greater need to maintain my defenses. But at the same time, I have a greater opportunity to break free from those defenses and allow myself to be known — just because we *are* so intimately related. What makes this self-disclosure so difficult, however, is that I don't really know myself all that well. Until situations like the one I just described come up, I am content with my self-constructed image of myself as a completely caring, considerate and respectful person, who wouldn't think of trying to take over someone else's life!

It has taken me some time to realize the value of having my shadow exposed. Early in our relationship a situation arose that threatened to put an end to the relationship. Elizabeth confronted me with something she felt I was withholding from her, while I could not see that I was withholding anything. The issue came up shortly before I left for my three-month stint in Japan, so I had plenty of time to sit with it. Gradually my resistances dissolved, until finally I could see what she saw. I didn't like what I saw, but I had to admit it was there all right. When I wrote to tell her that, I felt a burden had been lifted — and so did she when she read my letter. The fact that I had these "unacceptable feelings" was not as much a problem for her as that I denied having them. My openness cleared the way for her acceptance, which in turn made for greater trust on both of our parts. By facing the shadow in myself, I gained both self-knowledge and intimacy.

In praying with the psalms, I have sometimes asked God to "search me and know my heart."[5] I realize that nothing is hidden from God; nevertheless I ask God to search me and know the deepest secrets of my heart. Why? Is this not a way of asking for greater self-knowledge? How better to know myself than as God knows me? Yet how am I to come by this self-knowledge? Meditation, I am convinced, is one of the most effective ways we have of getting outside of ourselves in order to know ourselves — *even as we are known by God.* Another way, almost as effective, is through encounter with another person, preferably someone who is also a seeker and cares enough to serve as a mirror for our own self-understanding. Though it may not always seem so, this act of reflecting back what we see in another is a wonderful gift and true work of love.

The value of confronting one's shadow is recognized not only within the Christian tradition, but also within Buddhism. In the meditation group that Elizabeth and I attend, we sometimes recite a passage from Torei Zenji, an early Chinese Zen master. It reads, in part, as follows:

> How can we be ungrateful to anyone or anything?
> Even though someone may be a fool,
> We can be compassionate.
> If someone turns against us,
> speaking ill of us and treating us bitterly,
> it's best to bow down:
> this is the Buddha appearing to us,
> finding ways to free us from our own attachments —
> the very ones that have made us suffer
> again and again and again.[6]

What I especially like about this passage is the recognition that *anyone* can provide an occasion for facing our shadow, even our worst enemy. Bowing to the one who speaks ill of us or treats us bitterly is a way of recognizing the divine within him, but also a way of letting go of our attachments to ego. What we are attached to, it turns out, is a false image of self, which we need to let go of in order to be true to our *authentic* self. It can be painful to see oneself reflected in the eyes of another, especially someone we are close to, but it can also be liberating. Facing one's shadow is, in my experience, one of the most powerful ways of extending contemplative practice into daily life.

The Need for Time Alone

In June following our January marriage, Robert and I moved into the family cabin while awaiting the completion of our new home. One evening, after we'd been living in the cabin for several weeks, we found ourselves bickering over whether to set the alarm for 4:45 or 5:00 a.m. in order to arrive on time for an early-morning Zen sitting in

Colorado Springs. By the time we went to bed, I was feeling tearful and somewhat unstrung, and I asked myself what was going on. It was such a minor issue!

The next morning on our drive down Ute Pass, it occurred to me why I'd been feeling so contentious. My soul was crying out for private time! I think this is not an unusual thing for couples in their later years, especially those who have retired. In the spring and summer of our lives, we're busy with careers and family, and each has separate interests and activities that create built-in time apart. However, during the Autumn Years, there's more time for togetherness and this can be a true blessing. But it can also become a source of unnecessary friction if there's too much of it. We've found that it's essential to *plan for* time apart if it isn't readily available in the daily schedule.

Robert and I are fortunate to have a cabin, so we make it a point to take separate private days at the cottage on a fairly regular basis. But a quiet park or a library reading room or an open church may serve this purpose as well. We've also developed some individual interests. Robert has taken up gardening, so he spends quite a bit of time outdoors, which he thoroughly enjoys. He's also sometimes asked to give talks to various groups, so both of these things serve as time apart for us. I go into the city for a women's dream group once a week and I often have lunch with friends on other days. Both of us visit our families, sometimes separately, sometimes together. How much more we enjoy our time together when a few threads of private time are woven into the fabric of our lives! In this way, we encourage one another to develop our relationship with the indwelling divine.

Meditation has helped me to realize that we all need a certain amount of alone time in order to stay in touch with our inmost being and with our God, and I think this may be especially true for those of us living in our Autumn Years. Supporting each other's need for alone time is a vital way of supporting one another in our individual spiritual practices.

A Mature Sensuality

One of the loveliest surprises of marriage in the Autumn Years is a mature sensuality, an intimacy of vision and hearing and scent and especially touch that is so mutual that receiving is not separate from giving. Brother David Steindl-Rast, in his delightful book *A Listening Heart: the Spirituality of Sacred Sensuousness,* makes the very important point that enjoying our senses is not, as the Puritans supposed, a sinful thing. Our senses are, in fact, graces of incarnation, gifts of our embodiment in human form. "What a privilege for us to be alive in this period of history when more and more people are waking up to the realization that sensuousness is sacred."[7]

During the Autumn Years, it's natural to begin to notice some fading of the senses. Vision may become clouded, hearing is likely to be less acute, even the senses of smell and taste may begin to show signs of atrophy. But there is one sense that seems to remain fully alive: the sense of touch. This is especially precious now, when the others are fading, and there's a quality about it that isn't present with any other sense that makes it particularly valuable: it is impossible to *give* touch without also *receiving* touch. Robert and I enjoy giving each other massages, and we've noticed that it is just as pleasurable to be the one who massages as the one massaged. In fact, at some point the two merge, and it's hard to say who is the giver and who the receiver.

There's also something we can do to compensate for our fading senses of vision, hearing, smell, and taste. We can pay more attention to the sensory input we do have! Steindl-Rast suggests that we make a point of noticing at least one thing each day that feeds our senses and express gratitude for it. As a way of keeping himself focused on sensory input, he writes down, each evening, one sensory object he noticed and appreciated anew. I have begun practicing this, and have come to appreciate such ordinary things as the deep azure blue of the tiles above the pharmacy window as I've waited in line, the early-morning chirp of the chickadee outside the bedroom window, the crisp scent of pine logs crackling in the fireplace, and the delight of a single square of Hershey bar held in my mouth as it slowly melts.

There's also a lovely surprise in store for those who think that sexuality is lost to people past sixty. How pleasant it is to discover that, with the lessening of the urgency of youthful passion, comes the quiet joy of making love long, without the need to rush to a goal — just enjoying each other's bodies, taking joy in giving each other pleasure. Perhaps some couples in their Autumn Years who have given up the sexual part of their relationship might rediscover it in a new way by bringing in all the senses. Music, candlelight, aroma lamp, and massage can create a loving, pleasurable environment that reminds us of the sacredness of sensuality. Whereas earlier in life, sexuality may be thought of as something to do for a thrill, at this time of life it's more likely to be an expression of sustained love between two people. Waking up in the night (a common complaint of people our age) can be an opportunity to hold one another in the enveloping comfort of a long sleepy embrace. Enjoying sensuous pleasures together can be a spiritual practice of the Autumn Years, one that greatly enhances a couple's intimate bonding. It's a true blessing of this time in life.

Friendship and Community

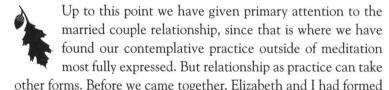 Up to this point we have given primary attention to the married couple relationship, since that is where we have found our contemplative practice outside of meditation most fully expressed. But relationship as practice can take other forms. Before we came together, Elizabeth and I had formed

several friendships with a distinctly spiritual dimension. She has spoken of her friendship with Jan, but there is also her friendship with Mona. It exhibits many of the qualities of intimacy we have been speaking about — openness, vulnerability and a shared concern for one another's spiritual growth. Even now, when they no longer live in the same town, they maintain their relationship by visiting one another when they can and at other times calling to talk about matters of special concern, usually having to do with a family situation, a book they have read together, or a dream one of them has had. My friend Richard and I have a similar relationship, though we see each other less often than Elizabeth and Mona. We communicate primarily by e-mail, but on several levels: intellectual, emotional and spiritual. From time to time "Richard" appears in one of my dreams. When that happens I can be almost certain the dream has a spiritual connotation. It is that kind of a friendship.

The "act of conscious attending to another person" that Jacob Needleman speaks of in the quotation that opens this chapter need not be confined to married couples. It can, and should be, an element in any genuine friendship. It involves, as he says, both "intentional listening" and "intentional speaking." Intentional listening, in which we set aside our egotistical concerns and consciously attend to the concerns of another, creates intimacy. It puts us in touch with ourselves even as it opens us to others, thus fulfilling a necessary condition for intentional speaking, which proceeds naturally from our true self, and not simply our socially conditioned self. There is great joy when that happens. In fact, "there is nothing in the world," Needleman contends, "that can take the place of one person intentionally listening or speaking to another."[8] The practice of meditation can prepare one for this kind of communication, but communicating in this way can also be an extension of one's meditative practice, a way of taking it out into the larger world.

Elizabeth and I see this especially in the spiritual community to which we belong. Our Zen meditation group, which meets several times a week in the chapel of Colorado College, is a lay community. We have no resident professional leadership, though we have two California-based teachers with whom we communicate regularly by phone and who come three times a year to lead retreats. For the most part we are on our own: sharing leadership responsibilities, developing and modifying procedures, and resolving conflicts as they arise. We like the freedom and fluidity of our little group, but like any community it has its problems. We all come from different places and bring different expectations to our common practice. For instance, some of us want to bow, when others would prefer not to; also, some would like to see leadership roles more clearly defined, while others are reluctant to see anyone given too much authority. So we do not always agree. In the absence of a clearly defined structure, we have found that communication is essential, but not always easy.

We have tried various ways of improving communication within the group. A regular monthly newsletter is one way; weekly announcements and a time for sharing at the conclusion of our Monday night sits is another. A monthly community night also helps us to know each other better. But these and other modes of communication, valuable as they are, lack the intimacy we seek. Recently a member of the group with experience in leadership training proposed a workshop in which those in leadership positions, along with a few from outside of the leadership, would come together for a day of intentional listening and speaking. The object was to gain greater clarity and consensus regarding our common purpose. We agreed at the outset that we would use loving speech, listen well, and speak from direct experience. We talked about what we do well as a group and what was not working well for us at the present time, and we brainstormed about where we would like to be five years from now.

Then we engaged in a unique form of group process called *visual exploration*. Several dozen pictures — some photographs and some reproductions of paintings — were scattered across the floor; we were each invited to walk among them and select two that particularly spoke to us of our community's purpose; then one by one we placed the pictures we had chosen in the center of the room and listened while others in the group responded to what they saw in the pictures. The idea was to allow creative insights to emerge, the sort of insights that would probably not come forth if we were operating strictly from the left side of the brain. It was, as it turned out, a very intimate process, in which everyone took risks and we all learned from one another. At the end of the day, we agreed that this shared experience had contributed significantly to our spiritual growth — as individuals and as a community. We saw it as an extension of our practice.

Opportunities for contemplative practice, I've decided, are to be found almost anywhere. We have only to bring a contemplative mind to a situation in order for it to become an occasion for practice. Sitting on your cushion, attending to your breath or invoking your sacred word can, and probably should be an important part of your practice, but it's not the whole of it. As Sister Maureen once said to me, meditation should serve as a platform for discernment. Discernment can occur anytime and anywhere, so long as we are open to what life has to teach us.

CHAPTER SEVEN

The Outer and Inner Journey

*In my picture of the world there is a vast outer realm and an
equally vast inner realm; between these two stands man, facing
now one and now the other.*　　　　CARL G. JUNG

Our friends the Pantles take separate vacations. David
journeys to places such as Peru, Bolivia, and Mexico
on birding expeditions, while Sherrill thoroughly enjoys
staying home and traveling within, through contemplation, music, reading, and just soaking up the joys of solitude. They
are always delighted when their journeys bring them together
again, to share all the richness of their respective travels. This
arrangement works in a wonderfully complementary way for them.

Since Robert and I enjoy both outer and inner journeying, we
have found a combined approach to spiritual excursion valuable
and mutually reinforcing, especially at this time in life. Earlier in
our lives, travel was often a matter of going to various places and
seeing as many sights as possible. Now traveling itself has developed a contemplative dimension for us that cannot be separated
from the places we visit. This is partly because our energy levels
have decreased and we simply prefer a less frantic pace, but it's
also due to our desire to walk together on a sacred path through
our remaining years.

The sense of *place as sacred space* has been part of our way of
thinking since childhood because of the fact that both of us have
always considered the area where we now live to have deeply

spiritual connotations for us. There are many places in the world that are widely considered to be spiritual energy centers, some of which we have visited, such as Stonehenge, the isle of Iona, and the Celtic pilgrimage sites of northern Wales. Yet wherever we might travel, even within our own state, can be an adventure into the spiritual, since our practice has imbued us with ways of carrying the contemplative spirit with us wherever we go.

Travel as Practice

Our first experience traveling together was our wedding trip to Plum Village, the community in the south of France founded by Thich Nhat Hanh, which we spoke of earlier. It is a rather primitive setting for a honeymoon, a cluster of old stone buildings that once served as a farming community but now houses approximately a hundred monks, nuns, and occasional retreatants like ourselves. We went there for the last two weeks of their winter retreat, when the weather can be quite cold, windy and rainy. We were advised to bring plenty of warm clothes and rain gear. Since it was our honeymoon, we decided to combine these two weeks in Plum Village with one week in Paris — and packed accordingly.

We thought we had planned well. Each of us had a regular-sized bag packed with extra-warm underwear, sweaters, ponchos, and several changes of clothes. We brought a duffel bag with our own sitting cushions, expecting many hours of sitting meditation and wanting to be sure we could sit comfortably. For the week in Paris, we packed a small bag with a few essentials we thought we might need in the city, such as dress clothes and shoes. Four pieces of luggage in all.

We were scheduled to fly out of Colorado Springs, change planes in Atlanta, and arrive in Paris the next day. From there we would fly to Bordeaux and take a train to the village of St. Foy la Grande, where we would be met by someone from Plum Village. We were advised to call ahead so they would know when to meet us. Unfortunately nothing went according to plan. Our departure from Colorado Springs was delayed by high winds, so we missed our connection in Atlanta. We were put onto a later flight, but when we arrived in Paris our luggage was nowhere to be found. So we spent the night in Paris and the next morning returned to the airport expecting to find our luggage waiting for us. Three of the four pieces of luggage were there, but the airlines had no idea what had become of the fourth piece, Elizabeth's bag with all of her clothes for the two weeks at Plum Village. We were assured that when the bag was found, the airlines would deliver it directly to our retreat site. Meanwhile she would have to make do somehow.

It was not a great prospect, but we were determined not to lose another day. So we took the next flight to Bordeaux, where we transferred to the railroad station and waited for the last train to St. Foy. By then it was dark and the platform where we waited for our train was dimly lit. It felt like a scene out of *Murder on the Orient Express*. When the train finally arrived, Elizabeth boarded first and I handed the luggage up to her. Then I realized to my horror that one piece was missing, the bag with my clothes for Plum Village! Looking around the nearly deserted platform, I couldn't see anyone who might have taken my bag by mistake. I reported the loss to the conductor, who shrugged, as only the French can, and told me the train was about to leave. Reluctantly I boarded the train and told Elizabeth that now we were both in the same predicament — facing two weeks without a change of clothes.

The train was barely out of the station when the conductor came up to me and said, "Did you hear that noise? I've never heard anything like it before. It sounded like the train just ran over a bag." There was a long pause; then I turned to Elizabeth and said, "Do you suppose the universe is trying to teach us something?" I received my answer several hours later when I called Plum Village to tell them that we had finally arrived. The woman on the other end of the line could no doubt hear the exasperation in my voice. In a quiet, gentle voice, she replied, "Just keep breathing." Our training in mindfulness practice had begun.

In Plum Village everyone practices all of the time. They have one particular practice that, as far as I know, is unique to their community, called the mindfulness bell. Whenever a bell rings — any kind of bell — they stop what they are doing and consciously breathe three times. If you are in the middle of a conversation and the clock strikes the quarter hour, you stop talking and breathe. If the phone rings, you don't rush to pick it up, as you might back home. You let it ring three times, while you patiently attend to your breath. Nothing is done in a hurry; everything is done mindfully.

In mindfulness practice you are letting go of attachments, all kinds of attachments, emotional as well as physical, in order to be fully present in the moment. By concentrating on your breath you facilitate the process of letting go and thereby create an opening for your larger Self to manifest. It is the small self, the ego, that wants to be in control, but in these magical moments when you let go of attachments you are released from that control into a state of true freedom and openness.

What I carried away from this experience was the realization that travel itself can be a form of practice. It is probably best to travel without too many expectations, since some of the most meaningful moments will come unexpectedly. The important thing, we have found, is to be mindful, attentive to whatever arises in the course of our travels. Sometimes it takes a disaster like lost luggage to get our attention, but more often it is the small, ordinary occurrences like a sea gull perched on a rock or the sight of heather on the hillside that touch us most deeply. If we are truly open — and that is what the practice is really all about — any new situation can be a contemplative moment, an occasion for wonder and gratitude.

Travel as Pilgrimage

Pilgrimage. It's a rather off-putting word, don't you think? At one time it called up for me images of ragged bands of pious people trudging along in the footsteps of "saints," hoping to suffer enough to be redeemed. Not a very inviting concept when seen in that light! And yet it is as old as human beings and a part of all the world's great religious traditions. Why do people travel to sacred sites? What are they hoping to find there? Andrew Jones expresses it beautifully in these words, "An outward pilgrimage is a sign of an inner journey — the journey of the heart which is held in the Creator's hands. It is rooted in the conviction that life itself is a process of continual change and movement."[1]

Several years ago, I read a book about a couple's pilgrimage to the isle of Iona, off the coast of Scotland, considered to be one of the world's "holy places," and I sensed I would someday make this pilgrimage. When I learned Robert had already been there and would love to return, we knew nothing could stop us. For us, I think it was a yearning to express in a concrete way the spiritual journey we shared. The actual pilgrimage was a six-hour hike over rocky, hilly, boggy terrain, to sites of special spiritual significance on the island, not an easy trek for a couple in their sixties at the time. Could we do it? Would we make it? I looked into my husband's eyes and read the answer: *Yes! We've come this far. We have each other. Together we can and will do it!*

The first thing we learned about pilgrimage was that it had to be a shared effort. Our guide Jan said that climbing over the slippery rocky surfaces would be treacherous and it would be essential for us to help each other there as well as in crossing the swampy bogs on the journey ahead. At a steep place between two jagged rocks, I struggled to get my footing. When I started to slip a young woman behind me said, "Let me carry your bag for you!" With her help I made it to the top of the mound.

Later, when we came to a boggy place, a long-legged man ahead of us leaped across and then reached back to help the rest of us make the long leap. A wondrous thing happened as people offered, and others accepted, help. We who had been strangers in a strange land became a bonded band of pilgrims traveling together as one body. This is one of the great rewards of pilgrimage.

Another lovely realization occurred when we stood on the highest hill and looked out over the water, where several other islands were visible. Our guide said that, though each isle looked separate, "if you go deep enough, you will see that these islands are all parts of a single landmass." This led Robert to reflect on his earlier visit to Iona when he climbed this hill and looked around to see water everywhere — a unique experience for someone who grew up on the plains of Kansas! It gave him a deep sense of solitude, but also a feeling of separation that was somewhat uncomfortable. Now he could see that there is a deeper unity that underlies the separation, and that felt very good. It is yet another metaphor for *interbeing,* the deep truth that, for all of our feelings of isolation and exclusion, we are joined in the unity of one Great Spirit. For us this is a contemplative realization, reinforced by the gift of pilgrimage.

Robert and I found this pilgrimage to be so spiritually enriching that we hoped to experience another sometime. About a year later we received an announcement entitled, "Soul-Filled Places: A Pilgrimage Embracing Christ's Presence in Celtic Wales." The words that really drew us in were: "You are invited to let go of the rhythm and control of daily life and experience an inward journey into God's presence, in the company of others. We hope you will join us!" Join them we did, with the greatest of joy. We

found the Llyn peninsula of north Wales to be a delightful place
of greenness, lavender heather and yellow gorse, rolling hills and
surging sea, and traces of the ancient Celtic people.

Celtic Christians, while believing that all things are sacred,
honor certain places as especially holy. They call these *thin spots,*
because there the line between time and eternity is veil thin.
A thin spot is a boundary place between the natural and the
spiritual worlds, a place where one can experience the vast boundlessness that is our true home. Wells are particularly honored as
places of healing. While we were in Wales, we visited a number
of holy wells. The one that felt most like a thin spot to me was
St. Seriol's Well.

In April, I'd had surgery on both my feet. It was now September, and my feet were still very weak, to the point that fellow
pilgrims often had to help me climb or pull me up after I'd fallen.
Sitting at the edge of St. Seriol's Well, I surprised myself by suddenly removing my shoes and putting my feet into the water! I'd
like to be able to say I was instantly healed, but it didn't happen
and I was disappointed. Then a university professor who spoke to
us that day called our attention to an interesting fact. The well
water looked absolutely still and yet it was clear as glass. Why
wasn't it stagnant? It was, in fact, coming from an underground
spring. The water was actually moving, even though on the surface nothing seemed to be happening. How like meditation that
is! So often, as we sit nothing much seems to be happening and
we may be inclined to give it all up. Yet Robert and I know from
our own experience that it is precisely during those apparently
fallow times that new growth is happening beneath the surface.
Sometimes it takes a contemplative pilgrimage to awaken those
seeds that have been just waiting to sprout!

Even though we visited many sacred sites on the Llyn Peninsula, the key destination of our pilgrimage was Bardsey Island,
just off the end of the peninsula. It's a quaint and peaceful isle of

monastic ruins, grazing sheep, a beckoning lighthouse, a sturdy mountain and a profound silence braided with the unhurried sounds of the sea. It is said that "twenty thousand saints are buried there" because the Celtic people believed that one would be res-urrected from the place of burial, and Bardsey was the most holy thin spot in Wales. Throughout the ages since then, visitors to the island have sensed a strong spiritual energy (both inner and outer) emanating from the land of Bardsey. So our sense of anticipation was brimming as the day approached.

Even though our group of twenty-four pilgrims had traveled thousands of miles over land and sea and spent two weeks on the peninsula leading up to our Bardsey crossing, we were told that we might not be able to make it to the island after all. Every-thing there depends on the wind, the sea and the grace of God. But on the day of our departure the sea was calm, and we were rowed in rubber rafts out to a waiting motor boat which carried us with great splashing wetness to our destination. I felt the island's special energy the instant I stepped off the raft that ferried us ashore.

Yet living conditions there were far from modern. We had learned ahead of time that there's no electricity on the island. Furthermore, we must boil the water for twenty minutes and then filter it to make it drinkable. And the clincher? No indoor bath-room facilities! All of this flipped a little anxiety switch inside me, especially the thought of getting up in the middle of the night to go outside! Yet despite my qualms, I found the gentle simplicity quite refreshing. At the end of our first day of silence on the is-land, Robert and I walked by moonlight back to our cabin, lit the candle in our room and got ready for bed. It was only 8:30 p.m. How long had it been since we'd gone to bed this early? But how long had it been since we'd known such peace, such inner still-ness, such a sense of commitment to each other and to the vast Unnamable?

We spent two days in silence on Bardsey, where we both had unusual and transforming experiences. You will read about one of mine in a later section; but the one I want to speak about now happened on our last day there, as Robert and I were walking back to our cabin. I was looking down at the rocky path when I suddenly stopped, breaking the silence. "I think I saw a stone with writing on it!" We retraced our path by three or four steps and I saw the rock again and picked it up. Scratched into it were these words: "It is all around you."

Who scratched those words into the rock? Who placed it there? How was it that I happened to see it, though others had walked by it without noticing? I decided to take the rock home as a reminder of this "thin spot" between time and eternity on Bardsey, as well as the thin spot that was now wide open within me. The rock now rests on our little home altar, reminding me that my everyday world is simultaneously the full expanse of the Great Vastness to which we all belong, and that pilgrimage is truly a gateway into both worlds.

Dream Work

So far in this chapter we've written about some of the ways that outer journeying can affect one's personal inner journey. But the reciprocity also works the other way, so now we'd like to discuss some of the ways that the inner journey can create changes in one's external life. We'll consider two forms of inner exploration: dream work and accessing one's inner wisdom through imagery.

I have been interested in dreams for as long as I can remember. While I was still in high school, I read Freud's *Interpretation of Dreams* and was astonished to find out what an active sex life I had. (Only in my dreams, of course!) There were times when my dreams portended some major change in my life, such as the dream that started me on the contemplative path, but most of the time they seemed pretty ordinary. Rarely would I discuss my dreams with another person, even my wife. I did not always understand my dreams, but I knew from my reading that dreams could contain hidden meanings that would be embarrassing if made public. So, for the most part, I kept them to myself — until I began seeing Elizabeth.

We discovered early in our relationship a mutual interest in dreams and took the risk of sharing our dreams with one another. Usually it would happen over the phone, but sometimes in correspondence, that one of us would talk about a dream he had recently had, only to discover that the other person understood it better than he did, or at least had some insight into its possible meaning that he did not have. We've carried this practice into our marriage, so that now every day begins with a "dream seminar" over the breakfast table. I may not remember a dream from the night before or may not think the fragment of a dream that I do remember is very important, but I have agreed to share what I remember. Invariably I find that there is more meaning in the dream than I initially thought. One of the rules of our dream seminar is that the dreamer always has the last word. Elizabeth may suggest a particular meaning or association, but unless her suggestion resonates with me it carries no weight. Also we try to avoid a lot of dream theory. We find that our best insights come when we stay close to the realities of our present lives.

I see my dream work as a way to attain greater self-understanding and ultimately self-integration. Though I greatly value consciousness, I think that much of our development takes place in the unconscious. There are various ways of accessing the unconscious, and Elizabeth will talk about one of those ways later in this chapter, but for me dreams — what Freud called "the royal road to the unconscious" — are the best way. At the time I started on the contemplative path, I began writing down my dreams. I do not write down every dream, but I do try to record the ones that make the strongest impression, what I call my *archetypal* dreams. They usually have a special feel to them, an aura of the numinous, as if they came from a place deep within my unconscious, as opposed to dreams that seem to be little more than a rehash of the previous day's events.

If you decide to work with your dreams, it is a good idea to write them down. It helps you to remember them and also allows you to go back and review them at a later time. Some people keep a pad of paper by their bedside so they can write down their dreams at the time they occur. I've done that on occasion, but usually I can remember my dreams well enough the next morning that I don't need to record them during the night. The important thing is to get down as much detail as you can. Dreams are usually very compressed, and every detail can be, and usually is significant. It is best not to interpret your dreams as you write them down; try to get an accurate account of the dream and save your interpretations until later. If you can discuss your dreams with someone close to you, I would encourage you to do so, since it will invariably lead to greater understanding on your part. The real meaning of a dream, as Freud recognized, is often initially hidden from the dreamer.

I keep a file of my dreams, which allows me to discern major developments in my unconscious. Thus, for several years following my retirement, I dreamt of returning to my previous job. I do not mean that I consciously longed to be back at the college where I had worked for seventeen years; rather my unconscious took me there in my sleep. At first I would dream that I had been offered my old job back: it seems they couldn't do without me! Later, I found myself back at the college as a consultant, and later still merely as an observer. By then I did not know anyone in the dream, and they did not know me. So I wasn't indispensable after all. The folks who had replaced me were getting along quite well without me. When I recognized what was happening in these dreams, how I was being gradually marginalized and eventually replaced, I realized how important my job had been to my sense of identity. It was no small thing to shuck off that identity. Even though I had made a conscious decision to retire, my unconscious needed time to absorb the change. These dreams were an indication of the progress I was making in assimilating this major life change and integrating it into my new self-understanding.

Jung saw the second half of life primarily as a time for what he called "individuation," realizing oneself as a complete person. For men this meant coming to terms with the feminine aspect of their psyche, for women the masculine. Both Elizabeth and I have seen this process at work in our dreams. Not long before we got together, she had a particularly powerful dream that spoke to her need to be more assertive by more fully integrating the masculine in herself.

In the dream, a man wearing an electric blue and green outfit comes to teach her a game. He is challenged by another man dressed in red. They struggle, and this frightens her. She tries to protect her granddaughter, who is by her side. The man in blue prevails and she realizes that she must join in the struggle.

Reflecting on this dream, Elizabeth could see that the man in blue represented her soul, her *animus,* and the game he came to teach her was the "game of life." Initially she was afraid for the child in her, but he showed her that she had the strength to assert herself in a situation where her integrity was at stake. By becoming more "masculine," I do not think she has become any less feminine; rather she is in the process of becoming a more complete person.

Some of my most persistent dreams in recent years have dealt with the feminine, though no one dream stands out in the way that Elizabeth's dream of the man in blue does. My feminine soul, or *anima,* is sometimes represented by my mother, other times

by my sister, my daughter or Elizabeth. It is as though my unconscious was seeking various ways of manifesting this complex
internal reality. Meanwhile, at the conscious level, I can see that
there has been development in the direction of greater individuation. Traditional feminine qualities, such as recognition of feelings,
appreciation for beauty, and expressions of love, have become
a more integral part of my life. As a result, I feel like a more
complete person. My dream work, I am convinced, has greatly
facilitated this process of inner and outer development.

There is yet another way that dreams can contribute to personal integration, and that is through *life review*. Sometimes I
think the primary purpose of a dream is to revisit some earlier
time in my life, perhaps "a road not taken" or a painful situation not fully appreciated at the time. I had such a dream on
the pilgrimage to Wales, immediately following our visit to Bardsey Island. It was one of the most extraordinary dreams I have
ever had.

I woke in the middle of the night *flooded with dreams*. It was
as though I had been watching several movies at once. I felt
I would lose the dreams if I did not immediately write them
down, so I took a pad of paper and began to write. Elizabeth woke up briefly and saw me writing. She went back to
sleep, but woke again thirty minutes later and was surprised
to see me still writing. Although I could not remember experiencing the dreams in sequence, that is how I wrote them
down. There were five distinct dreams in all. Reading what
I had written the next day and reflecting on the meaning of
the dreams, it seemed clear that they represented different
periods in my life and followed the order in which events
actually occurred. If there was a common theme running
through the dreams, it was my encounter with the feminine
at different times in my life. But there was more to it than

that. Each episode captured an important period in my personal development and confronted me with a new way of viewing it.

Looking back on this experience, it is as though, having traveled to a "place of resurrection," I returned to finds parts of myself that I had considered dead brought to life again and presented for review. While I don't expect to have another dream like this one, I have come to think that life review may be one of the most important tasks of the Autumn Years.

Accessing Inner Wisdom through Imagery

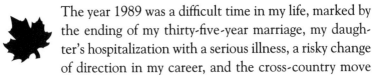 The year 1989 was a difficult time in my life, marked by the ending of my thirty-five-year marriage, my daughter's hospitalization with a serious illness, a risky change of direction in my career, and the cross-country move of my two closest friends. All of my external props were suddenly gone! Yet haven't we all found that it's during just such times of greatest stress that new ways of coping arise? At that time, I attended a two-week intensive workshop in a method of spiritual direction derived by Dr. Harold Edwards from Roberto Assagioli's concept of *Psychosynthesis*. This is a practical method of spiritual growth that embraces the soul as well as the mind, the imagination as well as the intellect, and the will as well as the instincts.

Two years later, I traveled to New York to be trained by Dr. Edwards and others in the Psychosynthesis method of providing spiritual direction to people seeking to discover and begin living their own deepest truths[2] What I discovered in this process is that you and I already have, within our own unconscious, everything we need for our own wholeness. One of the most effective ways of accessing this unconscious material is through the active imagination, which is "a technique developed by Dr. Carl Jung in which we have waking dreams or experiences of the imaginal realm while fully conscious."[3] Because the conscious mind must be awake to engage with the Wise Being who dwells within, "active imagination sets in motion unifying processes that link the ego and the unconscious to one coordinated whole."[4] In active imagination, the conscious and unconscious parts of the mind communicate with one another.

As part of the inner/outer journey, I'd like to lead you in an exercise directed toward putting you in touch with your own inner wisdom, through the use of active imagination.

Meeting Your Personal Wisdom Figure

It's necessary to find a quiet place and to allow at least an hour for this meditation so you won't feel rushed during the experience. Since I can't guide you in person, you may wish to tape record the meditation that follows, so you can play it back to experience it; or if you have a meditation partner, you can lead each other. In either case, pause for at least thirty seconds of silence after each item. Alternatively I'd suggest that you read through the meditation several times and then put the book down and follow the instructions as you remember them.

It's very important to be in a state of deep relaxation for this meditation, so I'll begin by asking you to lie down on a sofa (not your bed because you might fall asleep). Take a few long, slow, deep breaths, and then begin the following process of progressive relaxation. Begin by tensing your foot muscles as tightly as possible and then releasing them. Then do the same thing with the ankles, the calves, the thighs, hips, lower abdomen, solar plexus, chest, hands, lower arms, upper arms, neck, face, and scalp, tensing and then relaxing each group of muscles.

- Now take a few more deep breaths, close your eyes and imagine yourself to be in a beautiful meadow. It might be a meadow you've visited, or an imaginary one.

- Look around you and describe, aloud or silently, what you see.

- What does the grass look like?

- Are there flowers? If so, what color are they?

- Trees? If so, are they evergreens or deciduous or some of each?

- Is there water (a stream or creek)?

- What is to your right?

- Is there something to your left?

- Can you describe the weather?

- Are there sounds or scents?

- Now that you have a clear picture of your surroundings, ask that a Wise Being come into your meadow. Some people choose to invite Jesus, or Buddha, or Gwan Yin, or an angel, or other spiritual being; others prefer to let the active imagination surprise them with who appears. (The first time I did this meditation, the "wise being" who appeared was a hippie backpacker named Special!) Pause and allow plenty of time for this being to appear. You may actually see the figure in your mind's eye, or you may simply sense their[5] presence.

- Continue to pause until a being appears.

- Greet the being who has come and give them a chance to respond if they choose.

- Notice how the person is dressed, the expression on their face, posture, closeness to or distance from you.

- Wait and watch for a while to see what the being may do or say.

- Then, if you have a question, ask it and wait. The response may be immediate, or the wise being may want to silently deliberate before answering. It's also possible that they may show you the answer symbolically by what they do rather than by putting it into words.

- They might have a gift for you. If so, graciously accept it and thank them.

- You may also ask for an explanation of what the gift means, or for an elaboration on their answer to your question. Allow what happens to be.

- You might choose, now, to ask if there's anything this being would like from you. Again, wait patiently for a response.

- Ask any further questions you might choose to ask.

- Then thank this wise being for coming into your meadow today and say goodbye.

- After your wise being has left, look around your meadow to see if anything has changed. Perhaps something will have been added, or taken away, or the colors may have changed, or the weather might be different.

- Now gradually return to the room and take your time before opening your eyes and sitting up.

The very important final step is to write down everything you remember about the experience, along with any interpretations or insights that come to you as you write. It's essential to keep in mind, as you process the experience afterward, that the being who appears in your imagery is not Jesus or Buddha or an angel or a hippie backpacker. It is your own inner wisdom that is usually not accessible to the conscious mind. Thus the inner journey becomes an outer journey in a fascinating way. The fact is that the *unconscious* doesn't know the difference between an actual event and an inner one, though of course the conscious mind does.[6] This is why the gifts and insights received from one's inner wisdom figure can have a transforming effect on old patterns of thought and behavior that are no longer constructive.

Synchronicity

 In the quotation that begins this chapter, C. G. Jung expresses the view that the "inner and outer realms" are equally vast and that human beings, standing within both realms, face now one and now the other. Elizabeth and I have experienced this *vastness* in both our inner and outer journeys. We have found the two realms to be inseparable and profoundly interconnected. One moment we are in one, the next moment in the other.

When Elizabeth put her feet into the healing water of St. Seriol's Well, nothing happened outwardly, but then she learned that the still water of the well concealed an underground stream and suddenly realized that inner healing could be taking place without her knowing it. In that moment, the outer gave way to the inner. As for myself, Bardsey Island was outwardly a place of great stillness and beauty, yet it did not convey the spiritual energy for me that it did for others. Then, my first night back from the island, I was flooded with dreams, archetypal dreams from deep in my unconscious. So this thin spot turned out to be an opening to the inner realm after all. These are examples of movement from the outer to the inner, but the process can also run the other way as we have seen with dreams, which arise from the unconscious yet frequently portend major life changes, and the active imagination, which provides access to our inner wisdom for the purpose of transforming our lives.

Elizabeth and I are comfortable with being "now in one realm, now in the other," but we treasure those exceptional moments when we find ourselves simultaneously in both realms. Jung called such moments *synchronistic*. By synchronicity, he meant "the hypothesis that one and the same (transcendental) meaning might manifest itself simultaneously in the human psyche and in the arrangement of an external and independent event."[7] Since he coined the term it has made its way into popular speech, until now it is almost commonplace; yet it is not well understood. For instance, it is frequently used for events that are merely coincidental. You meet a friend in some unexpected place on your travels, and you think it must be synchronicity. Or you are thinking about someone, the phone rings, and it is that very person calling. These are certainly interesting occurrences, but they do not fit Jung's definition of synchronicity.

In order for something to be synchronistic, there must be both an inner and an outer event occurring simultaneously, without any causal relationship, yet manifesting a common meaning. The meaning, moreover, must be related to the *individuation* process we talked about earlier. In other words, it must contribute in some significant way to the individual's development as a complete person. Very few situations, even the most out-of-the-ordinary occurrences, fit that definition. Synchronistic experiences are relatively rare and regarded as special when they occur. I would like to think, however, that they occur with greater frequency for those who are on the contemplative path.

Our experience with lost luggage on the trip to Plum Village was, in my opinion, truly synchronistic. Anyone who has traveled very much has probably lost his luggage at some time or other. It is a great inconvenience, but not an occasion for deep reflection. There is usually a perfectly understandable explanation. In our case, the bags did eventually show up. It took awhile to reconstruct what had happened to them, but we came up with a plausible explanation. The particular constellation of events, first losing Elizabeth's bag and then mine under totally different circumstances, was certainly unusual, yet not in itself synchronistic. What made it synchronistic was the *meaning* it had for us. At the same time all of this was happening, we were on our way to a spiritual retreat, one purpose of which was to learn *to let go of attachments*. We were also beginning a new life together, traveling together for the first time, and looking for ways to develop spiritually: all factors related to our individuation. The inner meaning of the trip corresponded to what was happening externally, a sequence of events we could not possibly have anticipated and certainly did not cause to happen, while the two together — the inner and the outer — contributed in an important way to our spiritual development. It did not seem like such a great thing while it was happening, but once the meaning became apparent we realized that we had received a very great gift.

If you are on the contemplative path, you should expect to receive many such gifts. They may not all fit the definition of synchronicity, but they will almost certainly have both an inner and outer dimension.

CHAPTER EIGHT

The Contemplative Experience

We cannot lose our true home, our enlightenment, because it is right here, nowhere else. All we have to do is remember it.

JOAN SUTHERLAND

For me, one of the most valuable discoveries of these Autumn Years is that *all of us* are born with a jewel-like inner beauty that is normally hidden under delusions about who we "should" be, buried underneath all the roles we play, and covered over by the many layers of who we *think* we are. We are beautiful because we share in the Great Consciousness, that quiet Presence that dwells within as well as beyond our smaller selves, whispering: *You are so much more than you think you are!* This is the gate that leads to the practice of contemplation.

Although there are many forms of contemplation and meditation, the *experience itself* cannot be defined in a conceptual way. In the following section, I'd like to try, by way of metaphor, imagination, and koan to offer a taste of the beauty that awakens.

A Fresh Mountain Spring

It's a green and gold, pine-scented June morning in the 1940s in the little village of Green Mountain Falls, fourteen miles west of Colorado Springs. My father and I are making our usual hike to the spring, some fifteen minutes up the road from our summer cabin, to get our daily supply of drinking water. We spread apart the leafy shrubs that hide this place from the road and work our way down to the little stream that sounds like a bubbling fountain as it rushes over its rocky course. My dad opens the tall aluminum water container, gets down on his knees, and extends a large, long-handled dipper toward the natural rock wall. There it is, spouting out of the rock crevice as it has for a hundred years or more — *the spring.* Pulling the dipper back, he holds it to my lips for the first sip. *Mmm. Fresh. Crystal cold and thirst quenching. No faucet water ever tasted like this!*

"But why can't we just dip our water out of the creek?" I ask my father. He reaches down, scoops up a dipper full of stream water, and I see that it's full of sediment.

"The spring water comes from an underground stream," says my dad. "It's cold and clear because it's melted snow from the high mountaintops that has gone underground, invisibly following its purifying course for many thousands of feet, uncontaminated by man or beast."

As we walk back to the cabin, I keep thinking about that underground stream. It seems magical to my child mind, a newly discovered secret, a hidden reality beyond the one I've already known. And as the years of childhood pass, the idea of a deeper reality continues to grow within me, adding to the longing that reaches back as far as my memory can stretch.

During my spring and summer years, I continued to hike to the spring because being in that spot somehow connected me with that which was beyond myself. No matter how burdened I felt, no matter what heaviness I carried, no matter how alienated from myself I seemed, when I found my way to the spring, all the dammed-up tensions flowed out and I seemed to hear a voice echoing across the centuries: "The water that I shall give him will become in him a spring of water welling up to eternal life."[1]

It was as if, right there in that place, as well as right now in this place, with all of its physical sights and sounds and scents, there is another world that is just as real, though unseen and unheard. And the *spring itself* — as pure and flowing as the living water that Jesus offered, or as the Tao, or as the field of infinite possibility — is the link between the visible and the invisible! For me, the spring has become a metaphor for contemplation.

The circle of seasons has moved on and the time of my Autumn Years has come. The spring no longer pours forth from the rocks by the stream. But I have tasted of the Spring beyond the spring . . . the one that never runs dry. It is enough.

I've been reading, lately, about some of the new discoveries in physics and chemistry. They've caused me to take another look at the idea of the interpenetration of the spiritual and the physical. And the view is thrilling!

There's a marvelous book by the late world-renowned chemist Donald Hatch Andrews, entitled *The Symphony of Life*, in which he writes, "Science has pulled back the curtain and revealed that in the unseen and unheard there is a vast ocean of reality," and "what we see, hear, and feel accounts for *less than a millionth part* of the actual radiation and sound around us." Then he asks the reader to try to visualize what it would be like to see and hear these non-material sights and sounds.

Close your eyes for a moment. I wave a wand. Now look about you. The room is ablaze with dazzling light. The chairs, the tables — are prismatic crystals, sparkling with a thousand shades of red, yellow, green and blue such as you have never in your life seen before. Your clothes are on fire with a million microscopic flames. Your body is shining ruby, emerald and sapphire. The air itself sparks as if millions of miniature meteors are darting all about you.

In another wave of the theoretical wand, we hear a hurricane of sound like the playing of a thousand symphony orchestras. Every object in the room is booming, resonating, or trilling the most complex music.[2]

This is not fantasy! Of course, these colors and sounds are above and below the narrow limits which our senses can see and hear, but they are every bit as real as the sound of the bubbling water and the sight of the sun-etched leaf patterns on the ground here by this mountain stream. All of this makes it easier for me to know that spiritual reality is not some faraway, inaccessible thing, but that Spirit literally *permeates* physical reality. You and I are surrounded and infused by the Divine! This is the reality to which we awaken in the deeper levels of contemplation.

This morning on the mountainside, I can believe that the Divine, instead of being separate from this time and this place, truly indwells it, flowing like a stream in, around, and through me; and I know in some deep way that the natural world, underneath all its layers of grime and decay, is laden and shimmering with the sacred.

William Wordsworth knew it, too, when he wrote these lines above Tintern Abbey:

> And I have felt
> A presence that disturbs me with the joy
> Of elevated thoughts; a sense sublime
> Of something far more deeply interfused,
> Whose dwelling is the light of setting suns,
> And the round ocean and the living air,
> And the blue sky, and in the mind of man:
> A motion and a spirit, that impels
> All thinking things, all objects of all thought,
> And rolls through all things.[3]

It is this Presence that keeps me coming back, again and ever again, to this spring of contemplation.

There is a beautiful koan in the Zen tradition that speaks of a similar (or perhaps it's the same) spring:

> In a well that has not been dug
> Water ripples from a spring that does not flow.
> Someone with no shadow or form
> Is drawing the water.[4]

I love this koan because it touches the skirts of mystery. In the Zen lineage of our practice, there are no set answers or "right" interpretations to koans. They are meant to derail the logical, thinking mind so that the intuitive, expanding, freeing heart/mind can surprise us with fresh insights and openings. In fact, the same person may see something different in a koan each time she or he sits with it.

Please bear in mind that, to speak about it at all, I must resort to the use of concepts. However, the deeper treasure of the koan is not conceptual but experiential. One must hold a koan in the heart, in a state of not-knowing, drinking its mystery, as from a glistening mountain stream. With that caveat, I'll tell you how this koan appears to me on this day. I see the "well that has not been dug" as the field of infinite possibility, boundless and unknowable. The spring where "water ripples but does not flow" seems analogous to my mountain spring, representing the mind that has been brought to a still point in contemplation. Thoughts and feelings may drop into this "water," causing ripples, but the mind, remaining one-pointed, does not follow them. The One without shadow or form who is drawing the water is the Great Consciousness in which we all reside. Sometimes I have called this entity God, sometimes Holy One, sometimes *Anam Cara* (Soul Friend), sometimes the Divine, or the Source, or most accurately, the Unnamable. Now when I practice centering prayer, I use the name *Beloved,* for the Presence I meet in contemplation is most truly that.

The Underground Stream

I step onto the little weathered pine footbridge so I can get a better look at the spring water splashing down into the creek. As soon as it hits, it becomes part of the stream, so that it's impossible to tell where spring water stops and creek water begins. My eyes follow the creek until it curves around in front of John Morgan's house and disappears into the morning. But I know that it goes on...and on...and on, now above the ground, later underneath it. In fact, I've read that wells in eastern Nebraska pump water that has soaked into sandstone near the Colorado Rockies.

The encyclopedia tells me that water exists everywhere at some level beneath the surface of the ground. This water table is called an *aquifer.* I like to think that there is an underground stream of divine wisdom flowing everywhere below the surface of our limited human consciousness, and that there can be moments during this lifetime when we step into that stream and experience, for an instant at least, a reality that is beyond time and space. The point of entry may be a butterfly, or a sunset, or a symphony. It may be the welling up of praise from within, or a cry of the heart that knows its own insufficiency. And suddenly there is the knowing — the deep, sure inner verification of the fact that, though we live in a narrow physical world, we are part of a far vaster reality.

I experienced a glimpse of this reality when Robert and I were on our pilgrimage to northern Wales. As we began two days of silence on Bardsey Island, I found an inviting space by an old stone wall where I sat overlooking the fields and the infinite sea, and just allowed myself to sink into being. As I released the many small concerns of my daily life, I felt myself gradually entering into the great Oneness that is beyond naming. I became so absorbed in that unending vastness that I totally lost awareness of self. It was as if I *became* that great boundlessness. Some time later, I noticed that I was gazing deeply into a single blade of grass that was ready to spill its seeds, and I saw that it, too, was a mirror of the Great Consciousness. And it seemed, for those few minutes, that nothing existed but Love.

I don't want to give the impression that such experiences are available only to certain people or in special circumstances. They are not achievements, for there is nothing to achieve. Moments of unitive awareness cannot be *made to happen,* but meditation can help to prepare an opening in the heart/mind through which that unpredictable thing called *grace* may flow. Since all of us are already part of the seamless whole, it's only a matter of allowing ourselves to wake up to that wonder! And it can happen at any time — while one is ironing or doing boring paperwork or cleaning the bathroom, as well as on Bardsey Island or in St. Peter's Cathedral or a Buddhist temple.

In meditation, I can receive life-giving water from the boundless stream to sustain me during this journey through the wilderness of life. It can be my source of energy on those days when I'm exhausted and I'm sure I can't possibly go on...but the strength is there and I do. It can be the quiet reassurance that seeps up through my roots when I have to make a difficult phone call...and the right words come. It can be my guide in the loneliness of a heart-wrenching decision, even though I may still choose unwisely. Contemplation is not the answer to all problems. Life must still be lived, and life is sometimes messy and often difficult. But having wet my feet in those hidden waters, I know from experience that the stream is real and that I can trust its flow.

The Awakening Moment

 If anyone has been able to evoke the contemplative experience in words meaningful for our time, it has been Thomas Merton. As a young man he entered the most austere of Catholic religious orders with the intent of devoting himself exclusively to the contemplative life. He was prepared to give up the active life altogether, which for him meant ceasing to write, since writing was the career on which he had embarked. We can be grateful that his abbot did not see this renunciation as a necessary requirement of his religious vocation. Eventually he came to view writing as an integral part of his vocation, a way of sharing his contemplative experience with others.

One of his earliest books was entitled *Seeds of Contemplation.* Although written from the perspective of a monk, it found a wide audience among the laity, both Catholic and non-Catholic. Twelve years later he brought out a revised and expanded version entitled *New Seeds of Contemplation,* in which he acknowledged that his understanding had broadened and in some ways matured. "When the book was first written, the author had no experience in confronting the needs and problems of other men."[5] In the intervening years he had assumed the role of teacher and mentor to young novices who brought to him their loneliness, doubts, and confusions. He had also received numerous letters from readers who shared with him their longings and perplexities. Although he did not say so publicly at the time, he had also begun a study of other religions, notably Zen. What he found there so resonated with his own contemplative experience that he was moved to initiate a correspondence with D. T. Suzuki, a Japanese scholar who was at that time the best-known interpreter of Zen Buddhism to the West. In one of his letters to Suzuki, Merton confided that "if I could not breathe Zen, I would probably die of spiritual asphyxiation."[6]

The influence of Zen is clearly evident in the opening passage of *New Seeds*, where he addresses the question, "What is contemplation?" He writes:

> Contemplation is the highest expression of man's intellectual and spiritual life. It is that life itself, fully awake, fully active, fully aware that it is alive. It is spiritual wonder. It is spontaneous awe at the sacredness of life, of being. It is a vivid realization of the fact that life and being in us proceed from an invisible, transcendent and infinitely abundant Source. Contemplation is, above all, awareness of the reality of that Source.[7]

He realized that the word *contemplation* is subject to misunderstanding. It can raise in people's minds hopes that are "all too likely to be illusory, because misunderstood." Worse still, it can sound like a thing to be possessed, "something which, when possessed, liberates one from problems and from unhappiness."[8] That was not his intent, and neither is it ours.

For Elizabeth and me, as for Merton, contemplation is an *awakening,* an opening to the preciousness and sacredness of life, and with it the realization that "life and being proceed from an invisible, transcendent and infinitely abundant Source." We recognize, as he did, that this experience is not something to be achieved or, once realized, possessed. A person does not collect contemplative experiences as he might trophies, cars or antique furniture. One may pursue the contemplative path purposefully, as we have tried to do, but when these "special" experiences come, as they most certainly will, they invariably appear unexpectedly, like a sudden awakening from a dream when you didn't know you'd been asleep.

I will shortly speak of some of my *contemplative experiences,* since that is what drew me initially to the practice of meditation and helped to confirm me on this course, but I make no claims for their generality or replicability. No two persons' experiences are quite the same, I have found, yet there are sufficient similarities to allow for mutual recognition.

Seeing in a New Way

One of the first indications I had that meditation could make a difference was the way in which things I observed around me became more vivid and alive following several hours of sitting meditation. I recall, during one of my early five-day retreats, strolling in the garden outside of the retreat center and noticing how brightly colored and sharply delineated the flowers had become. It was as though I had been walking around in a fog without knowing it, when suddenly the air cleared. Everything — the blossoms, the leaves on the trees, each blade of grass, even the rocks — seemed more real and present to me than ever before.

I had a similar experience with respect to my fellow retreatants. Their faces were more clearly defined and expressive after we had been sitting together for several days than when we first came together. Since these retreats were largely conducted in silence, we had little opportunity to get to know one another in the course of a retreat. Yet I felt I could read their character from their faces in ways I cannot fully explain. For someone who does not easily remember faces, each face seemed extraordinarily memorable.

On one occasion, several days into the retreat, I had something like an epiphany. We were having lunch in the dining room, eating in silence as was our custom, when I looked up from my meal and was astonished to see that the faces of those across the table from me emitted a soft golden glow. Although none of them looked up, I sensed a profound sadness in their faces. I was overcome with a feeling of *compassion,* such as I had never known. The feeling was almost unbearable. In fact, I could sustain my gaze for only a few minutes before I had to look away.

Lest one suppose that these sorts of experiences happen only during meditation retreats, I want to speak of one that occurred outside of that context. It was probably the most profound contemplative experience I have ever had. It occurred quite unexpectedly during one of my visits with Elizabeth in the early days of our courtship. We are first cousins, so we had the advantage of having known each other since childhood. But there were major periods in our lives when we were not in touch and we needed to fill in those gaps if we were to enter into a new and deeper relationship.

On this particular occasion, we had spent the day together sharing intimate moments of our lives. It was late in the afternoon and the sunlight through the living-room window put Elizabeth's face in deep relief. She was talking about an especially painful time in her life, and there were tears in her eyes. I was sitting some distance from her, but I could sense the pain in her voice. Just as I was about to offer some words of reassurance, there was a shift in consciousness and I saw her in a new way: I saw her as a complete person, lacking nothing. In that moment I experienced what I can only describe as total, unconditional acceptance.

Maybe it was the effect of the sunlight at that time of day, but I don't think so. For a brief moment I saw clearly etched on her face lines of energy, similar to what one observes when iron filings are placed on a piece of paper and held over a magnet to reveal hidden lines of magnetic force. It was as though a veil had been lifted, and I could see beneath the surface of her face a profound inner strength. At the same time I had this feeling of unqualified acceptance. Yet to say that I *had* it would be misleading, for it did not seem that "I" was actually there. In that moment I was more of an opening through which the acceptance was manifest. On reflection I have come to see this experience as a manifestation of love, not romantic love in the conventional sense associated with "falling in love," or altruistic love of the sort that can inspire great acts of kindness on behalf of others, but a more radical form of love, what Christians call *agape*, a selfless love characterized by total acceptance of the other and typically ascribed to God. For me this was a grace-filled moment, in which God's love shone through me like the afternoon sun, revealing the hidden strength and inner beauty of my beloved.

Living with Ambiguity

 In the interest of wholeness, it's important that we present not only the joy and wonder of the contemplative experience but also its shadow side. Lest we give the impression that contemplation is all mountain springs, underground streams, and afternoon sunlight, let us now look at some of its darker aspects.

Meditation, because it attempts to still the conscious, thinking mind, tends to access the unconscious. Though this veiled part of the mind contains many beautiful memories, creative ideas, artistic sensibilities, and gems of the imagination, it also holds childhood traumas, unacknowledged fears and anxieties, "inappropriate" urges and desires, and sometimes even the seeds of psychosis. Therefore, there are a few people who would be best advised not to spend long hours in meditation. Those with a history of psychological problems probably should not begin the practice without first consulting their health care provider.

Having said that, I can add from my own experience that there seems to be something within me that "knows" when I'm ready to handle certain shadow material and when I'm not. For example, one evening during a very calm, peaceful meditation, an extremely painful and frightening memory suddenly burst forth into my awareness. It was of an early childhood incident in which someone I loved very much beat a dog to death. I had completely blocked this out for fifty years or more. Yet here it was, staring me in the face and demanding to be noticed. With it came all of the original horror and intense fear — fear even for my own life. I didn't try to get rid of the agonizing feelings but just sat with them and continued to focus on my breath. The adult Elizabeth didn't try to comfort the child or convince her it hadn't happened. Yet the adult *was there,* quietly observing and remembering ... and breathing ... in ... out ... in ... out ... and the meditation itself provided a kind of comforting wrap, like a mother's arms, from which to relive the experience.

This was not the end of it. I felt the need to confirm the memory with my brother, and he, too, had blocked it out. Yet the moment I brought it up it came back to him as clearly as it had for me. We talked about it for a long time, and found healing in the shared pain of it. The memory still comes back on occasion, and when it does it still hurts, but I think my meditation practice provides a softening field in which to continue processing it.

The fact is that life and suffering are inseparable. Young mothers do sometimes die; at this moment children in many parts of the world are being maimed by exploding land mines; and somewhere this night a young father will cry himself to sleep because he killed the man who raped his three-year-old daughter. It's true that children pull off the legs of frogs and gouge out the eyes of baby birds, and that otherwise loving fathers have been known to beat dogs to death. Yes. There is hatred and cruelty and irreparable sorrow in the world, and not even meditation can sweep it all away, because it's all mixed up with love and patience and compassion and the wonder of the starry sky and spring's first yellow crocus. And there is no separation. Slowly, with the help of meditation, I am learning to accept this — all of it — as the living, beating heart of life. We do not choose to have our hearts pierced, but pierced they become nonetheless, and out of our wounds flows the healing red fluid of compassion. We can learn to embrace the ambiguity. It's the wholeness we are.

Ordinary Mind

 The practice of meditation, particularly in a retreat setting over an extended period of time, can call forth experiences of extraordinary depth, beauty and poignancy, or as Elizabeth observes, moments of great pain and sorrow, but not all contemplative experiences are of that sort. Some are quite ordinary, woven into the fabric of daily life. It might be that moment when I saw snow falling on the deck of our house and felt that everything was just as it should be, nothing was lacking. For me in that moment the snowflakes contained the whole of reality. But it could just as well have been the time when, in the midst of a conversation, I backed our car into the side of the garage and ripped off the rearview mirror. That too was an awakening moment! Regrets and recriminations would come later, but in that moment the sound of crushing glass was the whole of reality.

Much of the delight of reading the journals of Thomas Merton comes from glimpsing through his eyes the immediacy of the world around him.

> Today has been beautiful. The sun shines, it is warm. There are neat little clouds up in the blue sky. The brown dirt is piled high on the grave of poor Brother Gregory, who turns out to have been Swiss. The reason why he used to limp was that one day a bull tossed him over a stone wall and nearly broke his back.[9]

Everything for this contemplative monk was alive and real, because it had not been filtered through the critical judgments, interpretations, and expectations we typically bring to our experiences. The sky is blue, the dirt is brown, and Brother Gregory limps because he was once thrown by a bull. That's it: nothing special, nothing lacking.

By the time we reach the Autumn Years we have acquired a great deal of experience, much of it distilled into prejudgments of various sorts. Some of these judgments are no doubt helpful in making our way in the world. They constitute acquired wisdom for getting things done and staying out of harm's way, but they can also interfere with our enjoyment of the present. What we bring to our experiences can enrich them, but also stand in the way of our experiencing life in all of its newness and freshness. There is, after all, a sense in which every moment is new. This very moment sitting in front of my computer and looking out the window has never existed before and will never exist again. I need to appreciate it for what it is, to be fully present in this moment. Meditation can help me do this since it is primarily a matter of letting go and clearing away rather than acquiring and possessing. Meditation can be valuable any time in life, but it is especially precious in the Autumn Years since this is the quintessential time for simplifying and appreciating. Zen Buddhists have a saying: "Ordinary mind is Buddha." Nothing more is really needed; it's all right here in this present moment if we will just wake up to it.

CHAPTER NINE

Some Fruits of Contemplation

We shall not cease from exploration.
And the end of all our exploring
Will be to arrive where we started
And know the place for the first time.

T. S. ELIOT

Autumn carries many associations, but for me it is particularly a time of remembrance, a time for looking back on the year drawing to a close and savoring all that it has brought forth. For our forebears, and many of the world's people who still live close to the earth, it is the harvest season, the time when they gather the fruit of their summer's labor and, if they are fortunate, lay aside a supply for winter. My mother used to can fruits and vegetables around this time of the year. Later when I had a garden of my own, I liked to pickle cucumbers and sometimes made preserves. These homegrown products of my own labor always tasted better than anything I could buy in the store, and were especially appreciated during the long winter months that followed. Now that I have come into my Autumn Years, I can see that this "season of life" can also be a time of remembrance, of taking account of what has been done and what remains to be done, of harvesting the fruits of a lifetime's experience and passing on to others what has been gleaned from that experience.

151

There is another association autumn has for me — a more mysterious, uncanny association. Fall is, as every child knows, the season of Halloween, when ghosts and goblins are said to appear. I have images of tombstones and jack-o-lanterns and going trick-or-treating in my neighborhood after dark. Halloween is a scary time for a child, but also a particularly fertile time for the child's imagination. You get to dress up in all sorts of wild costumes, pretending to be a hobo, Superman, a witch or a devil. All religions have something like this in their tradition, and it is celebrated about the same time of year. I am reminded of the "thin spots" in Wales, those places where the veil between the visible and the invisible is especially porous. Autumn is the *time of year* when the veil between worlds is thinnest, when we feel closest to those who have died and most vulnerable to unseen powers. It may also be a time when we are most receptive to the divine imagination.

I see the Autumn Years as *the time in life* when we are "moving between worlds" and therefore most open to the mystery of life and to the influx of divine images. It can, for that reason, be a very rewarding time made richer by contemplation. In this closing section, Elizabeth and I will talk about some of the fruits of our contemplative practice that we have begun to harvest at this time in our lives, and we invite you to join us.

An Inclusive Faith

Of all the gifts with which we humans are endowed, I think imagination is one of the most precious, and I have found that the regular practice of meditation enhances the expansiveness of that capacity because it opens a new willingness to be amazed. This again became glisteningly clear to me just a few weeks ago, when I received a rich-with-meaning gift of affirmation through a surprising image.

As you have read the story of the development of my personal faith, you have seen that I have struggled with, and to a large extent resolved, my early dilemma about combining Christianity and Zen Buddhism. For me, the Autumn Years continue to be a time for reassessing my faith and making it my own. I have let go of some of what I was taught in my formative years, developed a new appreciation for other aspects, and adopted some new ways of seeing and of practicing my faith. I have tested this inclusive path I have chosen, by living it, and it has proved to be solid. As St. Paul said, "When I was a child, I spoke like a child, I thought like a child, I reasoned like a child; when I became a man, I gave up childish ways."[1]

In giving up literal ways of seeing spiritual truths, I feel I have become more open to new and grace-filled insights. For example, on a recent morning in mid-September, I was startled awake by a sudden image that was gone almost as soon as it appeared. I sat up in bed with this surprising realization: *That was Jesus!* Though the image lasted less than a second, it remains, even now, amazingly vivid and detailed. It was not the suffering, feminized Jesus I had seen depicted in so many paintings, but a very strong, solid being. He was standing in a stream that ran from east to west, with a tall staff (not a shepherd's crook) in his hand and he seemed to be probing the bottom of the stream with it. The stream was in a deep ravine with tall cliffs on both sides.

This happened on the morning of the beginning of a Zen retreat. I had no idea what it meant, if anything. All I knew was that it had *not* come from my conscious mind. As I sat in meditation with it, I saw that this figure was not external to me but *within* me.

Two weeks later, an opportunity arose to meet with my former spiritual director, with whom I had co-led some retreats. Sister Sylvia Winterscheidt, CSJ, is an expert in the Jungian technique

of using the active imagination to explore the unconscious. I described the image to her and told her I had been practicing Zen.
She asked what I had received from my practice, and I replied
that it had brought, among other gifts, a much wider, more inclusive faith that was boundless and unnameable. She knew that,
some years past, I had developed something of a resistance to the
person, Jesus (for reasons having to do with my personal history).
In fact, as I said earlier, there came a time when none of the
names for God worked for me anymore. At that time, the gift of
the name *Beloved* came to me and it felt right and true. I told
Sr. Sylvia that, since I couldn't even say the name, Jesus, this
out-of-nowhere image was a *total shock*.

During the imagery session, I found myself walking with this
Being, whom I now saw as the unnameable Beloved, encom-
passing all that is divine, and his presence felt very strong and
supportive. We were moving eastward in the stream, against the
current. Sylvia remembered that the water was flowing from east
to west, and she said, "Didn't you just tell me about something
precious that had come into your life from the East?" *Of course!*
Zen. Why hadn't I thought of that?!

When I asked the Beloved what he was probing for with his
staff, he said he was trying to find where my grounding was. I had
been feeling some loss of self-confidence and the need for a more
assertive, stronger stance. In Jungian psychology, a dream of the
coming together of a strong male figure and a vulnerable female
one represents integration, wholeness, or the divine marriage between soul and spirit. I saw that I needed the internal masculine
to balance my life. In the final part of the session, as I was thank-
ing the Beloved for appearing to me in this way and walking with
me, he startled me by giving me a gift — his staff! Later I realized
that not only the image, but also the Beloved, was not external
but within me. I also saw that the gift of the staff was an affirming

symbol encouraging me to call upon my own inner masculine for strength and grounding.

In closing, Sr. Sylvia asked me to look around in my imagination to see if anything had changed. Yes! The cliffs had been replaced by flat land stretching out as far as I could see in all directions. This had happened as the Beloved and I walked eastward. Later, as I was recording the session in my journal, several things occurred to me.

First, I realized I hadn't left the Beloved behind after all, but that he was walking with me as I journeyed into the East to discover a new spiritual practice! As I was telling Robert about the experience he made another fascinating observation: the wide-open landscape that became clear at the end of the imaging session was in keeping with my earlier statement to Sr. Sylvia about the broader, more open view Zen had given me. And for the first time, I saw that this *includes* Jesus! And why not? Was there any reason this openness to all religions should *exclude* him? I saw that I had previously relegated him to a very narrow place (in the ravine, sandwiched between the tall cliffs) based on earlier misconceptions. Yet I now see that he, too, understands and loves the wider, more inclusive view. This whole experience was a confirmation from within me that the inclusive path I have chosen is *right* for my soul.

Yesterday I spent some time on the mountain behind our house looking for the staff in order to make the internal experience outwardly tangible. When I found what I knew to be the right stick (not surprisingly *by the stream*), I brought it home and placed it in our meditation room as a lasting reminder of this beautiful gift of the divine imagination, an imagination made fertile by contemplation.

Clearly, the Autumn Years are a time for making our faith our own, and possibly for allowing it to become wider and more all-encompassing. Perhaps, during this life season of the falling leaves, you might ask yourself: *Which of your beliefs are truly your own, what truths have you tested in your life and found to be part of the solid ground of your mature faith? Could it be that this is the time to reach for the ripe fruit of your personal authenticity of the spirit?*

Life Review

 In late February of this year I received word that my Uncle Howard had died. He was the last surviving male relative of my parents' generation. It was sad to know that he would no longer be around to pass along stories from the family history or share his dry wit and optimistic attitude with the rest of us. But he had lived a good life. He was within a week of being ninety-nine years old, and until the last few years was in very good health (walking into town every day, visiting with friends, occasionally playing a round of golf). I was therefore unprepared for my reaction to his death. Returning from his funeral, I broke out in a rash that would not go away. My doctor prescribed a medication that relieved the itch temporarily, but as soon as the medication wore off the rash was back. Visits to an allergist and a dermatologist failed to uncover a physical cause. I was forced to conclude that the cause was probably emotional and had been triggered by my uncle's death.

On reflection I could see that a significant shift had occurred: there was no longer an older generation to look up to. I was now on the frontline. Within a month the last remaining member of that older generation, my mother's twin sister, also died. I felt really exposed, as though the buffer between death and myself had been removed. Of course, I knew that any of us can die anytime, but somehow having a generation ahead of me gave me cover (or, at least, the illusion of cover). Now I would have to face the prospect of my own death, and for awhile I thought that was all there was to it. But the rash didn't go away.

Then I began to have dreams about my mother and realized that it had been five years since her death. Perhaps I hadn't fully acknowledged her passing and this was in some way a delayed grief reaction. I wasn't able to be with her at the time of her death, but I had spoken at her funeral, so I felt I had acknowledged her passing. Yet my body was telling me otherwise. The eulogy I gave at her funeral was in the nature of a public performance; perhaps what was needed was something more personal. But if so, I didn't know what form it should take.

The night before our fall meditation retreat, the same night that Elizabeth woke with her image of Jesus, I had a disturbing dream.

In the first part of the dream, I am trying to get to a wedding in the basement of a church, but the girl at the door won't admit me because I don't have a ticket. In the second part, I am directed upstairs and take a seat in the back row of a small, well-lit chapel. As I am sitting there, feeling uncomfortable, several large, open boxes containing grey-haired women laid out in formal attire pass slowly by.

My initial reaction to the dream — the second part anyway — was that it had to do with my mother's funeral. As for the wedding, it could represent the integration of my masculine and feminine aspects, something that is very important to me at this time in my life. Possibly, I thought, the dream is telling me that I cannot achieve full integration of the masculine and feminine until I let go of my emotional attachment to my mother. In other words, I can't get to the wedding until I first go to the funeral.

In discussing this dream with my Zen teacher, she noted that the wedding was taking place underground (presumably in the unconscious), while the funeral was above ground in the clear light of day. She suggested that the dream was calling for a *conscious* act of acknowledgment on my part. She didn't try to tell me what form it should take, but as I sat in meditation an idea emerged. I would take a trip in which I would visit some of the places where I lived with my parents when I was growing up, many of them places I hadn't seen in over fifty years. Elizabeth agreed to go along to help me process the journey as it unfolded. It would be a ritual journey, a *sacramental pilgrimage*, in which I would recall the many gifts my parents had given me, while at the same time releasing their hold on me — and mine on them.

The long contemplative drive across Kansas roads called back memories of my father, who was a resident engineer for the Kansas State Highway Department. During the first several years of my life, his job required that we move around a lot, so it would have been difficult for me to visit all of the places where we once lived. Instead I went just to those that had special significance for me. Fortunately my father kept good records, so I had actual street addresses for most of the places. I also had photographs to compare with what I found at these various places.

The journey proved quite fascinating. Heading east across Kansas, we went first to Oberlin, where following my birth Mother spent seven weeks with her parents; then to Phillipsburg, where she made friends with another young mother, a friendship which continued for the rest of her life; and then to Marysville, the first place of which I have an actual memory (I was about four at the time). As I stood in front of the house where we once lived, I felt very "protected" and sensed that it must have been a very happy time in my life. Here, and in several other places we visited, I burned a stick of incense to mark the occasion.

My family moved to Topeka shortly before I started school, and my parents soon decided to settle there, remaining in Topeka for the rest of their lives. We lived in several different houses during the time I was going to school, and I visited each of them in turn. I was sorry to see that the house where I lived the longest, a two-story brown shingled house on a large corner lot, was rather run-down. The yard in particular was not well cared for, and that was especially disappointing since I remembered how much care my father had given to it when we lived there. The next-to-last stop on our journey was Brewster Place, a retirement community where my parents spent their final years and eventually died. It was sad recalling those years of declining mental and physical health and realizing that I too faced the same prospect.

The next day we went to the cemetery where my parents are buried and placed flowers on their graves. Actually I brought plants from my garden in Colorado to put beside their burial place as a more personal expression of my love than something I might have bought. While we were there, I performed a ritual act of letting go by burning several of their letters and a birthday card I had saved. Elizabeth and I then said prayers on their behalf, and I once again burned incense in their memory.

On our return to Colorado, I composed a poem in the form of a Japanese haiku to express my feelings about the trip.

> In my autumn years,
> a longed-for journey home.
> The scent of incense.

What began as a way of completing the grief process became for me a "journey home," the expression of a deep longing I didn't know I had. Burning incense added to the experience by giving it a ritual quality and evoking a sense of the transience of life.

Looking back, I am especially glad that Elizabeth was with me on this journey. It was not only a healing experience for me but a bonding experience for the two of us. She has told me that she feels closer to me for having taken this trip with me and shared in some of my most precious memories. It is certainly appropriate that the trip took place in the fall as the leaves were beginning to change and a slight chill could be felt in the air. Autumn is the season of remembrance, when we feel closest to those who have gone before us. It is also a time of accounting, when we take stock of what has been accomplished and what is yet to be completed. *When you look into your heart, what do you feel remains to be done? What do you need to set right before the winter season of your life sets in?*

Leaving a Legacy

Being cousins, Elizabeth and I have a common set of grandparents. As we enter our Autumn Years, we find ourselves thinking more and more about this remarkable couple and the legacy they left. They belonged to the last wave of pioneers to settle this part of the country. In fact, our grandmother has written a personal account of the last Indian raid in western Kansas. They were the first in their families to attend college and were educators all of their lives. Our grandfather left the position of school superintendent in midlife to take over a grain and flour mill, but never stopped learning. One of my earliest memories is of his large library and the art objects he and Grandmother brought back from a trip they took to Europe in the midst of the Depression. Our whole family places a great value on education, largely because of them.

This legacy may seem rather intangible, but our grandparents also left behind some tangible gifts. One evening during the first year of our marriage, Elizabeth and I read to each other Grandmother Banta's family history. It is not the usual genealogy, limited to dates and names and little else. Her history is full of events and personalities, telling the story of the family's struggles with wit and warmth. We may not live up to her standard, but we are in our own way contributing to the family history.

For many years Elizabeth kept a journal and to date has accumulated enough journals to fill several boxes. Recently she began rereading her journals and extracting the parts she would like for her children and grandchildren to read, if they are so inclined. When my mother died, she left a box of photographs and memorabilia that she and my father had collected over the years (including a wedding invitation, birth announcements, newspaper clippings, and post cards from their travels). The box sat in storage for a long time, but then my daughter Jenny, whose hobby is scrapbooking, suggested that she and I collaborate on the creation of a Family Heritage Scrapbook. Putting this book together has provided me with yet another occasion for life review, while the book itself will become a part of my legacy.

Where we now live is on property that was once owned by our grandparents. It is where they came in the summer to escape the Kansas heat and where we used to vacation as children. There are on the property several large, stately spruce trees planted by our grandfather some seventy-five or eighty years ago. We have begun planting our own trees, knowing that they will not reach maturity in our lifetime but should be there for future generations to enjoy. I have also created what I call a "meditation garden" in a neglected corner of the property. We know better than to think that any of these plantings are permanent. One large forest fire could take it all away. But we believe it is important to think of future generations and to do what we can to leave a legacy that will connect the generations. *Have you thought about your own legacy? What fruits would you like to lay in store for future generations to savor?*

Living with the Mystery

 As Robert suggested earlier, there are things that need to be set right at this time of life. There are also things that we've tried to "fix" without success. Maybe it's time to let go of what is beyond our ability to resolve, entrusting these "impossible situations" to the great mystery of life. I have lived long enough to know that, even during times of terrible physical or emotional pain, Something has held me up, flowing through my life like a river, and that there is a transformational energy in pain, too. When difficult times arise (and they always do), I can look for the gold at the center of my heart and cultivate that.

Recently, in trying to learn to accept life's ambiguities, I thought of the double helix, the symbol for DNA. It's composed of two spirals that are really not two but one. While sodium (salt) passes through the membrane in a *downward* direction, glucose (sugar) is *ascending* the other gradient. It seemed to me that this, being the symbol for life itself, also represents the fact that living is always a braiding together of joy and sorrow, comedy and tragedy, loss and gain, and all the vicissitudes of human existence. As one aspect is rising, another is falling. And yet life is beyond these dualities. Wholeness involves all of it, and the Autumn Years are a time for embracing the ambiguities within the whole. To do this, life often asks us to let go of trying to control the movements of pain and joy, and simply accept what is.

For example, leaving Nebraska to live in Colorado was a truly heart-wrenching decision for me because two of my grown children and nine of my grandchildren still live there. It's part of my nature to be involved in my children's lives, even to the point of wanting to resolve their problems for them. This has not always been the best thing for them or for me, and such attempts are rarely successful anyway. Both Robert and I are separated, by distance or other reasons, from some of those we love, and there are times when the pain of that separation is quite intense, especially when they're hurting. We've found, however, that in meditation we can begin to let go of our need to solve the problems of our loved ones without losing our personal connection with them. In fact, meditation can actually *strengthen* our heart-level connection with them, creating a *new kind of intimacy* based on equality and mutual respect rather than on co-dependency.

It's the same with the global situation. Your grandchildren and mine have inherited a world full of suffering and violence. Every night, the news hour brings word of new suicide bombings; more soldiers and civilians killed in Iraq, Afghanistan, and other parts of the world; children and adults starving; and millions dying of AIDS. The world is undeniably in a state of extreme chaos and pain. We humans are rapidly depleting the earth's natural resources, polluting the air we breathe, creating global warming, and causing the hole in the ozone layer to grow, as well as destroying animal species and exploiting our few remaining wilderness areas. There are things I can do, such as recycling, writing to my senators and representatives, contributing to organizations working to reverse this ominous trend, and voting with this perspective in mind. Yet when I've done all I'm capable of doing, I need to open my hands and heart, trusting a Power beyond my small sphere of influence to take care of this fragile world I so dearly love.

Perhaps you, too, would like to ask: *Are there things in your life you have tried in vain to fix? Has the time come for you to let go and trust the divine (in the form most meaningful to you) to handle them?*

Endless Exploration

Though some mysteries need to be released, some simply need to be held. For example, I am still reeling from the wonder of some breathtaking synchronicities that occurred last Wednesday when I spent time on the mountain looking for my staff. I thought I had already extracted the full meaning from that surprising image of the Beloved. The insights I discovered through active imagination with Sr. Sylvia and input from others, as well as sitting with the question myself, are extremely valuable and will remain with me always. But the constellation of events on the mountain indicates there is more to be revealed.

First was the fact that my staff was lying next to the stream, as though waiting for me to come and pick it up. Then I found myself lost on a mountain I knew as well as my own breath, and my wandering brought me to a barbed-wire fence that required me to cross the stream. As I did so, I slipped on a mossy rock and found myself ankle deep in the stream, holding the staff I'd been given (just as in the image). Instead of panicking, I thought, *It's okay. I have my staff,* and within a few minutes I had climbed out and a house came into view with people standing on the deck. They were just ready to leave to go out to eat when I called to them. A young Japanese man named Hiro (pronounced *hero)* came down through the tangles of brush and led me to the house. As they offered to take me home, they mentioned they were a film team here from California to meet with a "script doctor," a woman who lived in the area. What they said next was a synchronicity too extraordinary to question. *The film they were working on was about the life of Jesus!*

Yet the mystery did not end there. Shortly after all of this happened, I received a gift. It was a book entitled, *Jesus, the Teacher Within,* by Laurence Freeman, with a foreword by the Dalai Lama. Again, the two religions were brought together in an integrated whole. Freeman asks the reader to hold the question posed by Jesus, "Who do *you* say I am?" As I have sat with this koan-like question, I am beginning to see it as another confirmation of the presence of the Inner Teacher, who is beyond the limits of any specific religion, the Beloved who refuses to be categorized. That's one answer, but I know it's just an opening into something greater than I am yet capable of fully understanding.

What I do know is that synchronicities, by definition, carry meaning and that when they occur they are a signal for me to pay attention! I will hold them in my heart, trusting that they will make their deeper meaning known to me in due time. And if not, I'll still hold them close, savoring the mystery itself. It is more than enough to last me through the winter season of my life!

There is also great mystery in those things I'd like to know before I die but probably never will. I'd love to know whether or not there is life on other planets; exactly what happens after the death of the physical body; what the lives of my children and grandchildren will be like when I'm gone; what new wonders will be invented in the twenty-first century; what the coming leap in consciousness (in which I truly believe) will bring forth; and so much more. All of my life I have asked unanswerable questions, and I hope I will never be so satisfied with the "answers" I receive that I'll stop asking. In the meantime, through meditation, I can relax into the great and enticing uncertainties of life.

Robert has also learned to love the mysterious. Lately he has been talking about building a little greenhouse in our backyard. He has been growing flowers for only a few years, but he is fascinated by the process and can see that it is an endless progression. Each spring brings new surprises as some plants survive and thrive, while others die out. He is even intrigued by the names of plants and is eager to add new ones to his list. I see no end to his explorations into the mysteries of growing things and other unfathomable aspects of creation.

Maybe you also have some unanswered questions to which the truest answer is *I don't know*. Can you simply hold them, embracing and cherishing the mystery, as you walk through these Autumn Years, continuing to explore? It's the contemplative way.

Albert Einstein has said,

> The most beautiful thing we can experience is the
>   mysterious . . .
> to know that what is impenetrable to us really exists,
> manifesting itself as the highest wisdom
> and the most radiant beauty
> which our dull faculties can comprehend.[2]

Notes

Chapter One / Flaming Colors, Falling Leaves

1. John W. Rowe and Robert L. Kahn, *Successful Aging* (New York: Dell Publishing, 1998), 4.
2. Ibid., 16.
3. Ibid., 21.
4. Ibid., 39.
5. Ibid., 46.
6. John O'Donohue, *Anam Cara* (New York: HarperCollins Publishers, 1996), 167.
7. Ibid., 178.
8. Stephen S. Hall, "Is Buddhism Good for Your Health?" *New York Times Magazine*, September 14, 2003, 46–49.
9. Ibid., 48.
10. Ibid., 49.
11. Ibid.
12. Rabindranath Tagore, *Gitanjali* (New York: Scribner Poetry, 1997), 61.

Chapter Two / Crossing the Abyss

1. George MacDonald, "The New Name," *Unspoken Sermons:* Series One (London: Alexander Strahan, 1867), 100–117.
2. Name changed.

Chapter Three / Interfaith Pilgrims

1. Marilyn Morgan Helleberg, *Beyond TM: A Practical Guide to the Lost Traditions of Christian Meditation* (Ramsey, N.J.: Paulist Press, 1980). Reprinted by Walker and Company, New York, under the title: *A Guide to Christian Meditation*.

2. The monastery, established by the Holy Cross Fathers and Brothers, offered retreats and workshops to Christians of all denominations.

3. For more about the relationship of these two spiritual leaders, see my book *Thomas Merton and Thich Nhat Hanh: Engaged Spirituality in an Age of Globalization* (New York: Continuum International, 2001).

Chapter Four / Finding Your Own Practice

1. Song of Songs 2:3–4, *The New Oxford Annotated Bible with the Apocrypha: Revised Standard Version* (New York: Oxford University Press, 1977), 816.

2. Thich Nhat Hanh, *The Miracle of Mindfulness* (Boston: Beacon, 1987), 11.

3. Ibid., 14.

4. Sharon Salzberg, *Lovingkindness: The Revolutionary Art of Happiness* (Boston: Shambhala, 1995), 21.

5. These are the classic statements that have been used by Vipassana meditators for centuries.

6. Jelaluddin Rumi, cited by Salzberg in *Lovingkindness*, 78. I heartily recommend Sharon's book!

7. Thomas Keating, *Open Mind, Open Heart: The Contemplative Dimension of the Gospel* (New York: Continuum International, 1995), 20.

8. Marilyn Morgan Helleberg, *Where Soul and Spirit Meet: Praying with the Bible* (Nashville: Abingdon, 1986).

9. John Tarrant, *A Guide to Sitting and Walking Meditation & Koan Starter Kit* (Occidental, Calif.: Pacific Zen Institute, 2003), 4.

Chapter Five/ Supporting Your Practice

1. Romans 12:5, RSV.

Chapter Six/ Relationship as Practice

1. Ehei Dogen, *Shobogenzo*. Dogen was a twelfth-century Japanese Zen Master who founded the Soto sect.

2. A. H. Almaas, *The Pearl Beyond Price* (Berkeley, Calif.: Diamond Books, 1988), 81.

3. Ibid.

4. Stephen Seijaku Roshi, Pine Wind Monastery, Shamong, New Jersey.

5. Psalm 139:23, RSV.

6. From Torei Zenji, *Bodhisattva's Vow*, trans. Joan Sutherland and John Tarrant.

7. David Steindl-Rast, *A Listening Heart: The Spirituality of Sacred Sensuousness* (New York: Crossroad Publishing Company, 1999), 43.

8. Jacob Needleman, *A Little Book on Love* (New York: Doubleday, 1996), 44.

Chapter Seven / The Outer and Inner Journey

1. Andrew Jones, *Every Pilgrim's Guide to Celtic Britain and Ireland* (Norwich, England: Canterbury, 2002), 3.

2. Harold Edwards, *Training in Spiritual Direction: A Psychosynthesis Approach* (©Harold D. Edwards, 1973).

3. Jeffrey Raff and Linda Bonnington Vocatura, *Healing the Wounded God* (York Beach, Maine: Nicolas-Hays, 2002), 153.

4. Ibid., 154.

5. You may use the pronoun appropriate to your wise being. Since I don't know that person's gender, I'll use the (grammatically incorrect) plural pronoun to avoid the awkwardness of such combinations as "he or she."

6. Harold Edwards citing Jung.

7. C. G. Jung, "Synchronicity: An Acausal Connecting Principle," *Collected Works*, vol. 8 (Princeton, N.J.: Princeton University Press, 1978), 482. Quoted in Victor Mansfield, *Synchronicity, Science, and Soul-Making* (Chicago: Open Court, 1995), 37.

Chapter Eight / The Contemplative Experience

1. John 4:14, RSV.

2. Donald Hatch Andrews, *The Symphony of Life* (Lee's Summit, Mo.: Unity Books, 1966).

3. William Wordsworth, "Lines Composed above Tintern Abbey" (New York: W. W. Norton & Company, 1975), 578–79.

4. Number 11 from *The Miscellaneous Koans* collection of Pacific Zen Institute/Open Source, compiled by John Tarrant and Joan Sutherland, 1996).

5. Thomas Merton, *New Seeds of Contemplation* (New York: New Directions, 1961), ix.

6. *The Hidden Ground of Love: Letters of Thomas Merton*, selected and ed. William H. Shannon (New York: Harcourt, Brace, Jovanovich, 1985), 561.

7. Merton, *New Seeds of Contemplation*, 1.

8. Ibid., x.

9. Thomas Merton, *The Sign of Jonas* (New York: Harcourt, Brace, 1953), 83.

Chapter Nine / Some Fruits of Contemplation

1. 1 Corinthians 13:11, RSV.

2. Albert Einstein, cited in Virginia W. Bass, ed., *Dimensions of Man's Spirit* (Los Angeles: Science of Mind Publications, 1975), 201.

Resources for Taking the Contemplative Path

On Aging Well

Martin, William and Chungliang Juang. *The Sage's Tao Te Ching*. Marlowe & Company, 2000. An innovative interpretation of this ancient Taoist classic adapted to the Autumn Years stage of life and written in a pithy style that invites reader identification.

Omega Institute, *Conscious Aging: A Creative Spiritual Journey*. Boulder, Colorado: Sounds True Audio. An album of six inspiring audio tapes from a conference on aging, including talks by Rabbi Zalman Schachter-Shalomi, Maggie Kuhn, Bernie Siegel, Ram Dass, and Marion Woodman.

Rowe, John W. and Robert Kahn. *Successful Aging: The MacArthur Foundation Study*. New York: Random House, 1988. Offers surprising facts about the preventability and reversibility of physical and mental decline in the elder years.

Schachter-Shalomi, Zalman. *From Age-ing to Sage-ing: A Profound New Vision of Growing Older*. New York: Warner Books, 1997. Rabbi Zalman's earthy spirituality encourages readers to live to the fullest and to pass their wisdom to future generations.

Woodman, Marion. *The Crown of Age: Rewards of Conscious Aging*. Boulder: Sounds True, 2002. A well-known Jungian analyst makes the point that as physical strength wanes, spiritual strength can grow. Drawing on her own and her clients' experiences, she leads the listener in dream work, imagination, and reflection to self-awareness and wholeness of the soul.

On Contemplation/Meditation

Anonymous Fourteenth Century author. William Johnston, ed. *The Cloud of Unknowing*. New York: Image Books, 1973. Probably the best introduction to Christian meditation for the serious spiritual seeker.

Freeman, Laurence. *Jesus the Teacher Within*. New York: Continuum International, 2000. Focusing on Jesus' question, "Who do *you* say I am?" Freeman sees deep listening and self-knowledge as gates that open into true relationship with God and meditation as the prayer practice that unlatches those gates.

Keating, Thomas. *Open Mind, Open Heart: The Contemplative Dimension of the Gospel*. New York: Continuum International, 1992.

———. *Intimacy with God*. New York: Crossroad, 1994. Father Keating is the leading interpreter of centering prayer for our time, and these two books are clear and forceful presentations of his approach to contemplative practice.

Merton, Thomas. *New Seeds of Contemplation*. New York: New Directions Books, 1962. A mature work of spiritual reflection by the most influential Christian mystic of modern times.

Nhat Hanh, Thich. *The Miracle of Mindfulness: A Manual on Meditation*. Boston: Beacon, 1987. A lucid presentation of the practice of mindfulness by a world-renowned Buddhist teacher and social activist.

Rohr, Richard. *Everything Belongs: The Gift of Contemplative Prayer*. New York: Crossroad, 1999. A Franciscan priest and founder of the Center for Action and Contemplation, Father Rohr shows how one can bring a contemplative perspective to all aspects of life.

Salzberg, Sharon and Joseph Goldstein, *Insight Meditation: An In-Depth Correspondence Course*. Boulder: Sounds True, 1996. An album of twelve tapes, each offering both meditation instruction and guided meditation in the Vipassana tradition.

Suzuki, Shunryu. *Zen Mind, Beginner's Mind*. New York: Weatherhill, 1970. Taken from talks given over a period of many years, there is no better introduction to classic Zen meditation than this little book by the founder of the San Francisco Zen Center.

On Interfaith Experience

Dalai Lama. *The Good Heart: A Buddhist Perspective on the Teachings of Jesus.* Boston: Wisdom Publications, 1996. A deeply spiritual interpretation of the Beatitudes, parables and other teachings of Jesus by the world's most revered Buddhist teacher and leader. Interfaith dialogue at its best.

Kennedy, Robert. *Zen Gifts to Christians.* New York: Continuum International, 2000.

————. *Zen Spirit, Christian Spirit: The Place of Zen in Christian Life.* New York: Continuum International, 1997. These two books represent major contributions to the current Buddhist-Christian dialogue by a Jesuit priest with authentic experience in both religious traditions.

Norris, Kathleen. *The Cloister Walk.* New York: Riverhead Books, 1996. A moving account of a Protestant woman's experience of the contemplative life during a year spent with a Benedictine community in Minnesota.

Steindl-Rast, David. *A Listening Heart: The Spirituality of Sacred Sensuousness.* New York: Crossroad, 1999. Utilizing both Christian and Zen sources, Brother David makes a beautiful case for the spiritual value of the senses, especially the deep listening of contemplation that fosters gratitude and intimacy with God.

Walsh, Roger. *Essential Spirituality.* New York: John Wiley & Sons, 1999. Drawing on a wide array of religious traditions, the author presents practical ways to enrich one's life through contemplative practice.

On Spiritual Growth

Johnson, Robert. *Inner Work: Using Dreams and Creative Imagination for Personal Growth and Integration.* San Francisco: HarperSanFrancisco, 1989. For those interested in exploring the unconscious, there is no more practical introduction to dream interpretation and active imagination.

Kelly, Thomas R. *A Testament of Devotion.* New York: Harper & Row, 1941. A Quaker perspective on the contemplative life, blending the mystical with the practical in a way that is deeply personal yet fully accessible to persons of other religious traditions.

Mansfield, Victor. *Synchronicity, Science and Soul-Making.* Chicago: Open Court, 1995. A brilliant treatment of the much talked about but frequently misunderstood subject of synchronicity, showing parallels with Buddhist philosophy, Jungian psychology and quantum physics.

Needleman, Jacob. *A Little Book on Love.* New York: Doubleday, 1996. A refreshing view on mature and lasting love as involvement of two people supporting each other's spiritual search and soul growth.

O'Donohue, John. *Anam Cara: A Book of Celtic Wisdom.* San Francisco: HarperCollins Publishers, 1997. Written from a contemplative perspective, this book will charm, delight, and deepen the reader's practice of the sacred in daily life.

Tarrant, John. *The Light Inside the Dark.* San Francisco: HarperCollins, 1998. A brilliant exploration of the psychology of the spiritual life from the perspective of both Jungian psychology and Zen.

Finding a Retreat Center

Housden, Roger. *Retreat: A Time Apart for Silence and Solitude.* San Francisco: HarperSanFrancisco, 1995. Not only does this book describe the various *types* of retreats available, but it provides names and addresses of various retreat centers as well as photographs of each center.

Most contemplative organizations also offer retreats and can provide information regarding retreat centers.

Organizations Supporting Contemplative Practice

Center for Action and Contemplation, P.O. Box 12464, Albuquerque, NM 87195.

Contemplative Outreach, P.O. Box 737, 10 Park Place, Butler, NJ 07405.

Insight Meditation Society, 1230 Pleasant Street, Barre, MA 01005.

Spiritual Eldering Institute, 970 Aurora Ave., Boulder, CO 80302.

Upaya Zen Center, 1404 Cerro Gordo, Santa Fe, NM 87501.

The World Community for Christian Meditation, International Centre, St. Mark's, Myddelton Square, London EC1R 1XX.